PIONEERS AND PATRIOTS

The aim of Zenith Books is to present the history of minority groups in the United States and their participation in the growth and development of the country. Through histories and biographies written by leading historians in collaboration with established writers for young people, Zenith Books will increase the awareness of minority group members of their own heritage and at the same time develop among all people an understanding and appreciation of that heritage.

ZENITH BOOKS SERIES CONSULTANTS

John Hope Franklin
Chairman, Department of History, University of Chicago

Shelley Umans
Director, Center for Innovation, The Board of Education of the City of New York

ZENITH BOOKS ADVISORY BOARD

John Gearon
High School Social Studies Consultant, Chicago Public Schools

Rayford W. Logan
Professor of History, Howard University

Gordon McAndrew
Assistant Director, The Learning Institute of North Carolina, Rougemont, North Carolina

Joseph E. Penn
Supervising Director, Department of History, Public Schools of the District of Columbia

J. Rupert Picott
Executive Secretary, Virginia Teachers Association

Isadore Pivnick
Coordinator, Federal-State Projects, San Francisco Unified School District

Samuel Shepard, Jr.
Assistant Superintendent, St. Louis Public Schools

Hugh H. Smythe
United States Ambassador to Syria

C. S. Whitaker, Jr.
Professor of Political Science,
University of California at Los Angeles

DR. JOHN HOPE FRANKLIN, Chairman of the History Department at the University of Chicago, has also taught at Brooklyn College, Fisk University, and Howard University. For the year 1962–63, he was William Pitt Professor of American History and Institutions at Cambridge University in England. He is the author of many books including *From Slavery to Freedom, The Militant South, Reconstruction after the Civil War,* and *The Emancipation Proclamation.*

SHELLEY UMANS is Director for the Center for Innovation for the Board of Education of the City of New York, a specialist in reading instruction and a member of the instructional staff of Teachers College, Columbia University. For more than ten years, she has been a consultant to many major urban school systems throughout the United States. She is the author of *New Trends in Reading Instruction* and *Designs for Reading Programs.*

LAVINIA DOBLER is Head Librarian at Scholastic Magazines. She has taught in her native Riverton, Wyoming, and in California and Puerto Rico. Among her numerous books and articles are *Customs and Holidays Around the World, Cyrus McCormick: Farmer Boy,* and *Arrow Book of the United Nations.*

WILLIAM A. BROWN is an historian who has specialized in the history of Africa. He is the recipient of a Foreign Area Fellowship which has taken him to Africa for further research and study.

DR. PHILIP CURTIN is Professor of History at the University of Wisconsin and head of the African Studies Program at the University. His latest book is *The Image of Africa.*

YVONNE JOHNSON is a designer and illustrator of books for young people. She did illustrations for the *Golden Treasury of Knowledge,* and is the designer for the *Crowell Collier 1964–65 Year Book.*

Benjamin Banneker

Paul Cuffe

Phillis Wheatley

Peter Salem

Jean Baptiste Pointe de Sable

John Chavis

PIONEERS
AND PATRIOTS

THE LIVES OF SIX NEGROES OF THE
REVOLUTIONARY ERA

Lavinia Dobler and
Edgar A. Toppin
Illustrated by Colleen Browning

ZENITH BOOKS
DOUBLEDAY & COMPANY, INC., GARDEN CITY, NEW YORK

The Zenith Books edition, published simultaneously in hardbound and paperback volumes, is the first publication of *Pioneers and Patriots*.

Zenith Books edition: 1965

CONTENTS

PIONEERS AND PATRIOTS

CHAPTER 1

BUNKER HILL HERO
Peter Salem

Peter Salem was puzzled. Why was his master so cross and impatient these days? Peter had tried not to displease him. If only he were a free man, and not a slave! Maybe his master, Major Lawson Buckminster, would tell Peter what was troubling him. Other leading citizens in Framingham, Massachusetts, seemed as tense as his owner.

As the months went by, the tension mounted. Peter noticed that many more citizens looked grave and worried as they walked along the tree-lined streets.

Then one day, in April 1775, Peter was in the garden near the big brick house, clearing the ground for the spring planting. Suddenly he heard Major Buckminster's sharp voice. It was high and strained.

"The British are unfair!" he exclaimed. "Why can't they realize we have our rights, too?"

Peter stopped digging and listened closely. Major Buckminster and a neighbor were standing by the picket-fence gate.

His master continued. "We should not have to pay taxes on goods unless we agree to that extra charge!"

Peter Salem

He spoke with determination. "Taxation without representation cannot go on!"

Peter had never before seen his master so disturbed. Even though he did not fully understand the meaning of the words, he realized this must be serious. This must also be the reason so many citizens were worried.

Peter heard the neighbor say: "We have shown our displeasure. Remember the Boston Massacre? We will never forget that March day in 1770."

"Or Crispus Attucks," Peter's master added quickly.

Peter shuddered as he recalled the tragic event when Crispus Attucks, a Negro slave from his village, was shot by British soldiers. Crispus was a strong man, Peter remembered, tall and big-boned.

There had been a clash between the British and the colonists over their rights as Englishmen. The Americans had resented the taxes they had to pay on essential items that came by ship from England. A group of men had heckled some British soldiers. A rioting mob had assembled in the streets of Boston, and the redcoats had fired on them. Five colonists were killed. The people of Massachusetts were indignant about the Boston Massacre, and the citizens in Peter's village were even more disturbed because a man from Framingham had been shot.

Now Peter heard the neighbor ask anxiously, "Then you are expecting more trouble between the British and the colonists?"

Major Buckminster lowered his voice. "Farmers and tradesmen already have hidden guns and ammunition. They will be ready when it happens!"

The neighbor caught his breath. "Then we're going to fight!"

"Yes." Major Buckminster paused. "But we'll need hundreds—thousands of soldiers."

"We have loyal men right here in Framingham," the neighbor said. "They'll fight, but they aren't trained soldiers."

As the days went by, Peter Salem heard more about these Minutemen. These were men who promised to be ready on a minute's notice to drop their plows, pick up their guns, and fight to defend their homes. On village greens across New England the Minutemen were drilling, preparing for action.

Excitement mounted. Peter was impressed with the patriotism of these Minutemen.

"Why can't I be a Minuteman?" he asked himself. "I want to fight to protect my village." He was strong and in good physical shape. He was young, too, only twenty-five.

Peter had heard that Negroes had served in the wars with the Indians, and in other conflicts between the British and the French. But he could not offer his services without his master's consent.

One day after Peter Salem had watched some Minutemen marching with rifles over their shoulders, he returned to the house, determined to ask his master for permission to join the Framingham company. Major Buckminster was a very patriotic man, so he probably consented cheerfully to Peter's enlisting.

Peter Salem was enrolled in Captain Simon Edgell's company of Minutemen. There were seventy-five men, all from Framingham. The company roll shows that

Peter Salem served four days with this company, from April 19 through April 23.

What memorable days those were to be!

Peter Salem was among the Negroes who fought on April 19, 1775, at Lexington and Concord, where was fired "the shot heard round the world." These were the first battles in the American Revolution that lasted from 1775 to 1783. It is not known how many there were, but Negro Minutemen and militia, or state army, volunteers fought for the Americans.

When the English general, Thomas Gage, sent a force under Lieutenant Colonel Francis Smith to arrest colonial leaders and seize their arms and ammunition stored at Concord, the Minutemen turned out to oppose the British. They had been warned by Paul Revere and Will Dawes on their famous midnight ride.

After getting the alarm, some seventy armed Minutemen, under Captain John Parker, met the British advance party under Major John Pitcairn at Lexington. Among them was at least one Negro, Prince Estabrook of West Lexington.

Two Framingham companies of Minutemen, Captain Edgell's and Captain Micajah Gleason's, hastened to Concord some fifteen miles or more to the north. Peter Salem and the other soldiers covered the distance in about two hours. Unfortunately there are no details on Peter Salem's role in the fighting at Concord. But some of the Negroes who fought that day were Minutemen Cuff Whittemore, Cato Wood, Pomp Blackman, and Lemuel Haynes. Prince Estabrook was a casualty in the battle at Concord.

Between the fighting at Lexington and Concord in

April and the famous battle at Bunker Hill in June other Negroes took part in fighting in May 1775 at Ticonderoga. Several Negro soldiers, including Primas Black, Epheram Blackman, and Lemuel Haynes, were with Ethan Allen's Green Mountain Boys when they captured Fort Ticonderoga in New York.

When Great Britain finally realized that the rebellious colonists intended to battle for their rights, the mother country started sending additional forces and officers from across the Atlantic Ocean to assist General Gage, commander of the British forces in the thirteen colonies.

By mid-June, General Gage had about 6500 men to oppose the colonists surrounding him in Boston. The colonists had been adding to their forces, too. They had some 10,000 men.

The stage was set for the Bunker Hill battle when General Gage and his officers decided to occupy Dorchester Heights, southeast of Boston. This was planned for June 18, 1775. When the rebellious colonists learned of this on June 15, they decided on a countermove. They would occupy Bunker Hill on the Charlestown Peninsula, on the north side of Boston.

The American commander, General Artemus Ward, ordered the Massachusetts regiments of Prescott, Frye, and Bridge, and various other units to enter Charlestown Peninsula, and to fortify Bunker Hill. Colonel William Prescott was in charge.

On the night of June 16, this force of 1200 men entered the Peninsula and began work. There had been several hours of debate among the officers. Some said that Bunker Hill should be fortified. Others insisted that Breed's Hill should be fortified. Breed's Hill was nearer Boston.

Finally the officers decided to fortify Breed's Hill and then build a second line of defenses for reinforcements and for a line of retreat on Bunker Hill. The men worked through the long dark night. Fortifications were finally completed by dawn of June 17, 1775.

After serving with Captain Edgell at Concord, Peter Salem had joined a company in the 5th Massachusetts Regiment led by Colonel John Nixon. He and the other men, who had had meager training as soldiers, now rushed to the scene as reinforcements as the battle began.

When the British discovered, in the early dawn, that the American rebels fortified Breed's Hill, they began immediately to bombard it from the water. There was not much damage because their ships were too far away.

The main American position was a redoubt, a temporary sort of fort, built on the side of Breed's Hill that faced Boston. To protect this, the town of Charlestown lay below Breed's Hill to the right of the redoubt. To the left of his position in the redoubt, Colonel Prescott had instructed his men to build breastworks, low, hastily-built walls of earth, to complicate a British attack from the side. The breastworks were built while the British unsuccessfully shelled the area.

By driving the men hard and ignoring the British shells, Colonel Prescott got the breastworks finished before noon. The rest of this left flank, or side, was protected by fortifications and a rail fence near the beach. Several hundred yards back of the fence, General Putnam waited on Bunker Hill with reinforcements.

The British decided to dislodge the Americans. Their forces under General William Howe landed at Moulton's Point on the Charlestown Peninsula about one o'clock in the afternoon of June 17. The redcoats started for Breed's Hill. The British officer had planned a frontal assault, while the main attack would sweep the left flank. But the Americans had strengthened the left flank since Howe's plan had been made earlier that morning. So the flank assault bogged down and the frontal assault was smashed by withering fire from American fighters in the redoubt.

While the British were landing on the Peninsula, reinforcements were coming up to aid the original 1200 tired colonists who had built the fortifications. The Massachusetts regiments headed by Brewer, Little, Scammon, Gerrish, and by Nixon were sent over to aid the defenders. The redoubt on Breed's Hill where the main fighting took place was defended by soldiers from Nixon's regiment along with Colonel Prescott's regiments and others.

There can be no doubt that Peter Salem participated in the Battle of Bunker Hill. He may have been in the redoubt throughout the battle. He may have fought in the earlier assaults from behind the breastwork on the redoubt's left flank and then been sent into the redoubt during the last assault.

Howe's second assault was directed primarily at the redoubt. But the forces were hurled back.

The people of Boston watched the fighting from the rooftops.

"We have many brave men!" they shouted. "Keep up the good work."

A third assault was begun by the British. The Americans were running out of powder. The men could not pour heavy fire into the enemy.

Prescott's men fought valiantly, fighting hand to hand, even after the British stormed the redoubt. The heaviest casualties for the Americans came when they finally retreated from Breed's Hill, back to Bunker Hill, and then across the narrow Charlestown Neck back to General Ward's headquarters at Cambridge.

The smoke from the burning of Charlestown and the confusion of the British forces closing in from three sides and fearing to shoot each other, let most of the men in the redoubt escape, including Peter Salem.

Colonel Nixon was wounded and carried from the field in the third assault.

Word passed quickly from one soldier to the other.

"Colonel Nixon has been wounded!"

"He can't leave us," Peter Salem shouted. "We need him." His Minutemen fought even more furiously.

As the British stormed the redoubt in the last stages of their third and successful assault, Major John Pitcairn, in his bright red uniform, mounted the redoubt to urge his men on. He was shot by a Minuteman. Who fired that shot?

Numerous accounts claim that Peter Salem killed the British major, thus having the distinction of becoming the hero of Bunker Hill! One historian, Samuel Swett, wrote:

Peter Salem shoots Pitcairn

"Young Richardson of the royal Irish, was the first to mount the works, and was instantly shot down; the front rank which succeeded shared the same fate. Among these . . . Major Pitcairn, who exultingly cried 'The day is ours,' when a black soldier named Salem shot him and he fell. His agonized son received him in his arms and tenderly bore him to the boats."

Swett also noted: "A contribution was made in the army for this soldier [Peter Salem], and he was presented to Washington, as having performed this feat."

Josiah H. Temple of Framingham described Peter Salem's part.

"During the action, he [Salem] with others, was sent from Capt. Drury's company, as a support to Col. Prescott in the redoubt. He reached the redoubt just as Prescott's men had spent their last powder; and with a single charge in his gun, and perhaps another in his powder horn. Just then, in the language of Judge Maynard, 'I saw a British officer . . . come up with some pomp, and he cried out, "Surrender, you . . . rebels!" But Prescott . . . made a little motion with his hand, and that was the last word the Briton spoke; he fell at once . . . this shot was fired by Peter Salem.'"

On the 82nd anniversary of the Battle of Bunker Hill, (which was really the Battle of Breed's Hill) the nation's great orator, Edward Everett, delivered the main address June 17, 1857, in Boston. Speaking of the great Bunker Hill Monument, Everett said:

"It commemorates no individual man or State . . . No name adorns the shaft; but ages hence . . . will perpetuate the memory of the 17th of June. It is the monument of the day, of the event, of the battle of Bunker Hill; of all the brave men who shared its perils—alike of Prescott and Putnam and Warren—the chiefs of the day, and the colored man, Salem, who is reported to have shot the gallant Pitcairn as he mounted the parapet."

Peter Salem had enlisted in the 5th Massachusetts Regiment on April 24, 1775, straight from his service as a Minuteman. Despite the fact that Negroes had served with state militia and had fought in the early battles of the war, America was debating whether to use Negro troops at the very time such a courageous man as Salem was volunteering to fight. Many people were opposed on principle to arming Negroes. The Continental Army, formed in June 1775, and commanded by George Washington, sought to exclude them from service.

First, a council of war held by Washington in July issued an order instructing recruiting officers not to enlist any more Negroes. Those already in the Army—Peter Salem being one—were not affected. But no additional Negroes would be permitted to join up.

Then, in September, an attempt was made to drop Negroes who were then in the service. Edward Rutledge of South Carolina introduced such a resolution at the Continental Congress, but it was rejected. Two weeks later, however, General Washington's council of war did vote unanimously to exclude slaves. It was also decided by a majority vote to reject free Negroes. Finally, on October 31, the quartermaster general was instructed not to permit Negroes to re-enlist.

How dismayed Peter Salem must have been to think

he would not be able to serve any more when his eight-month enlistment was up.

This order did not remain in effect very long. The British had already started to recruit Negroes. They offered freedom to slaves who enlisted in the British forces. The Governor of Virginia, Lord Dunmore issued a proclamation to this effect on November 7, 1775.

When Washington and others learned that Virginia slaves were flocking to the British side, they became alarmed. Also, free Negroes who had served protested the exclusion order. There is some irony in the fact that this order to exclude Negroes on the American side came two weeks after Phillis Wheatley, a Negro poetess from Massachusetts, sent Washington a poem praising him as Commander.

Washington wrote John Hancock, president of the Continental Congress, telling him that the free Negro soldiers were displeased at being excluded. Washington explained that he was re-enlisting them but would stop if Congress ordered it. On January 16, 1776, Congress approved re-enlisting the free Negroes, but stated that no new colored volunteers would be accepted. This made it possible for Peter Salem to re-enlist.

Wartime pressures and a scarcity of white volunteers eventually changed the policy, so that before the end of the Revolutionary War, the Continental Army and the states, except for Georgia and South Carolina, were accepting Negro soldiers, both slave and free. Generally, in both the northern and southern states, slaves gained their freedom by enlisting. Slaves were first enlisted in

Rhode Island early in 1778 at Washington's request, at which time Massachusetts also began taking slaves.

Most Negro soldiers in the Revolution served, as did Peter Salem, in integrated units. There were a few all-Negro regiments—two in Massachusetts and one each in Connecticut and in Rhode Island. Some five thousand Negroes served in the Revolutionary forces. Most of Peter Salem's service was with Colonel Thomas Nixon's Massachusetts regiment, and several sources refer to him as often serving as the colonel's body servant, as well as serving as a fighting man.

Peter Salem fought in the Revolution from its beginning in 1775 until near its end, or later, serving at least until 1780, and possibly until 1782.

By the time the Revolutionary War was over, Peter Salem, now a free man, felt very much a part of this new country known as the United States of America. He was proud that he had helped the country become free.

But having been a soldier for more than five years, he was eager to have his own home and settle down.

Peter Salem married in 1783 when he was about thirty-three. He built a small house on land near Sucker Pond in Framingham, but one historian reports that his marriage was not a happy one. Peter later left his native town and settled in Leicester, in central Massachusetts.

Peter earned his scanty living by making and mending baskets, and putting reed bottoms in chairs. Because of the kind of work he did, he went to many homes. He had an easygoing way, and because of his good nature, he was a favorite with the people of Leicester, especially the children.

Peter would tell the children stories of the war and what he had seen.

Boys and girls would beg him for a story, while he was mending the chairs. Other times he would sit in the chimney corner with the youngest on his knee, and while the flickering blaze lighted his face, he would tell the children stories of the war and what he had seen "when I was with Massa Nixon."

Because he was proud to have been a soldier in the American Revolution, he liked to tell about the exciting experiences at Concord and also on Breed's Hill.

"The British weren't as brave as we were," he told people, shaking his head. "They were not fighting for the same reason that we were. We were fighting for freedom." Then his voice would reach a high note. Once again he would be reliving those exciting battles of 1775.

Peter Salem especially looked forward to visiting other soldiers who had served in the American Revolution. He once told a friend: "I feel I will never grow old as long as my comrades remain to answer the roll call."

But Peter did grow old and too feeble to earn a living. According to the custom of the time, a person no longer able to support himself must be supported by the town he came from. It was a sad day for Peter when he had to leave his friends in Leicester and return to Framingham.

His former master, Major Lawson Buckminster and Captain Jeremiah Belknap, along with Samuel Hemenway, gave a bond to the town guaranteeing to support Peter for the rest of his life. In their eyes, he was no ordinary poor old man.

Today there is a memorial in Framingham, set up by

the local chapter of the Sons of the American Revolution, which bears the following inscription:

PETER SALEM

A soldier of the Revolution
Concord
Bunker Hill
Saratoga
Died, August 16, 1816

On patriotic holidays, the flag of the country he helped make possible floats above Peter Salem's grave.

CHAPTER 2

FATHER OF A CITY
Jean Baptiste Pointe de Sable

There have been many Negroes among America's discoverers, pioneers and explorers. Negroes accompanied many of the early Spanish and French explorers in the United States lands. Pedro Alonso Niño of Columbus' crew may have been a Negro. Nuflo de Olano was among thirty Negroes who helped Balboa discover the Pacific in 1513. The most renowned of early explorers was Estevanico (Little Stephen) who led an advance party in Coronado's quest in the southwest for the Seven Cities of Cibola. This was in 1540. In modern times, Negro Matthew Henson was with Robert Peary when he discovered the North Pole in 1909.

But one among them stands alone in founding a great American city.

Accurate information about the background and early life of Jean Baptiste Pointe de Sable is difficult to obtain. Accounts written during his lifetime only refer to him as a Negro. However, it is thought that he may have been born in Haiti about 1745. There is also considerable disagreement about his parents, but it seems likely that de Sable's father was French and his mother a Negro.

Jean Baptiste Pointe de Sable

It is not definitely known, either, when de Sable came to the Northwest. But he had the good fortune of being a friend to the Indians. His trading activities, friendships with them, and widespread contacts indicate he was probably in the West even before 1773. The fact that he was dark, more their color, and not white, like the pale-faced men, was to de Sable's advantage.

His color was not the main reason the Indians liked him. They knew they could trust him.

At one time he lived in an Indian village. He learned their ways of surviving, and they taught him how to trap.

He seemed to know many of the tribes, from the Gulf of Mexico to Canada, including the Illinois, the Ottawas, the Kaskaskias, and other tribes. He seemed, however, to be more at home with the Potawatomi.

He married an Indian woman, Catherine, in a tribal ceremony about 1771. He had been adopted by her tribe.

Did de Sable have any Negro friends? Several historians claim that Jacque Glamorgan, a Negro from Haiti, was his good friend. Glamorgan was a leading merchant of Spanish Louisiana who took the lead in exploring the upper Missouri and combating British traders. But he was not a Negro. He later became one of the first judges of the U. S. Court of Common Pleas at St. Louis.

If de Sable was Glamorgan's close friend, it shows that the Chicago pioneer had the qualities to win the friendship of men of responsibility. At one time de Sable may have had business experience in Haiti, then

De Sable was considered a friend by the Indians, not only because his skin was dark but because they knew they could trust him.

came to Louisiana, and associated with Glamorgan in the fur business in the St. Louis area.

There is also disagreement about de Sable's training. A British officer who knew him, refers to de Sable as being "well educated." Other sources indicate de Sable's "penmanship was limited to writing his initials."

There is an entry in the 1784 daybook records of the Detroit merchant, James May, showing de Sable had entrusted some of his personal effects to May's care. These articles included twenty-three paintings such as Lady Strafford, King and Rain, Love and Desire. They might have been Governor Sinclair's, the owner of the Pinery Post where de Sable was the agent. They are listed, however, as belonging to de Sable. If de Sable owned them, they show cultural tastes of a well-educated man.

Another piece of evidence is the bill of sale listing items sold to Lalime by de Sable in 1800 when he gave up his post at Chicago. The items include "1 cabinet of French walnut, 8×4 with 4 glass doors," and also "2 pictures." Having such items in his home might indicate that de Sable appreciated the finer things.

No doubt it was while trapping for animals on the plains and in the wilderness as well as in rivers and streams, that de Sable came upon the huge lake. Surely, he thought, many rivers drained into it. He was right. There was also a stream at the mouth of the lake, which would prove most useful.

Here was the ideal place to set up a trading post, the best he had found in his travels in this wild, beautiful country. Deer and other animals were grazing nearby.

They did not seem afraid. This meant that hunters did not come often. There seemed to be a great deal of wind in this area, but de Sable didn't mind. The French were in Canada, far to the north, and to the east people from England had settled on the Atlantic seaboard. De Sable had heard that many pioneers were moving farther west. But now, at least, de Sable would not have to worry about too many people.

He turned to his companion, an Indian from the Peoria tribe. "This is to be my trading post. It is a good place." De Sable made the symbol for good in the Indian sign language. "We can go by canoe well to the North. We are not far from the Illinois River or the Mississippi. We will not have to transport our hides too many miles across land."

The great lake we now call Lake Michigan. The city which grew up on the site of de Sable's trading post is, of course, Chicago.

From the days of the first French exploration of the Mississippi Valley, the site of Chicago was significant. It was the location of one of the most important portages, overland crossings between waterways, to the land of the Illinois and the Mississippi waterways.

The shallow prairie stream, that was later to be known as the Chicago River, was of great value because the narrow watershed between it and the Des Plaines River, that drained into the Mississippi through the Illinois River, offered an easy portage for explorers, fur traders, and missionaries bound for the great central plains.

The first white men to use the portage were Père

"This is to be my trading post. It is a good place."

Marquette and Louis Joliet. When they returned to Canada from their exploration of the Mississippi in 1673, they learned of the portage from the Indians, and found that it shortened their trip a great deal.

After Marquette, came other Jesuit missionaries, and then La Salle, who in the winter of 1682–83 first built a stockade at the portage. The Indian Mission of the Guardian Angel was established there in 1696 by Père Pinet. In spite of the strategic location of the mission, no French settlement developed there in the eighteenth century. Bitter hostility between the French and the Fox and Sauk Indians made the Chicago route a dangerous one. Fur traders of the middle Mississippi Valley made Kaskaskia, far to the south, below the mouth of the Missouri, their headquarters, and used the Ohio Valley instead to go to and from Quebec and the Illinois country.

De Sable, however, was able to run a successful trading post at Chicago. The Indians trusted him. His post flourished because they brought him their best grade of pelts.

However, life was not always smooth for this pioneer, for this was the time of the American Revolution. The American colonists were being aided in the West by the French from Canada and by the Indians. Once de Sable was driven from his Chicago trading post by the British. He had to move his home and trading business to Michigan City. Later he was arrested by the British and held for some time because they thought he was aiding the French and Americans.

During his time in prison, de Sable impressed the British officers. Major Sinclair, the commander of the fort where he was held, went several times to see de Sable in his cell. The major was amazed at this man's knowledge of the frontier west and even more impressed by the fact that he spoke excellent English as well as French.

Apparently de Sable won the confidence of Sinclair, who shortly released him. Sinclair had charge of a large trading post on the St. Clair River, a few miles south of the present site of Port Huron, Michigan.

The Indians, who traded at this post, became angry at François Bellecour, the Frenchman who was in charge.

The following summer after de Sable had been arrested, a band of Indians came to Mackinac to complain to the governor about the Frenchman. They asked that Bellecour be dismissed. They wanted to deal with de Sable.

"He is good. He is our good friend. We trust him," one tall Indian said.

Thus de Sable, who had for a time been a prisoner of the British, managed the important British trading post, the Pinery, from the summer of 1780 to the spring of 1784.

Old records indicate that de Sable had bought a farm at Peoria, Illinois, in the early 1770s. It seems likely that he began the Chicago trading post in the mid-1770s. He probably settled his wife, son, and daughter in Chicago while maintaining the Peoria farm and also running trading posts at Michigan City (1779) and the Pinery (1780–84). He finally concentrated his energies at Chicago from the mid-1780s until 1800.

In 1800, de Sable sold the Chicago post to Jean Lalime of St. Joseph, Michigan. It had been thriving for
two or three decades before he sold out. Why did he
sell? Perhaps he was tired of business, or perhaps the
area was becoming too developed for this pioneer.

De Sable was proud of what he had accomplished in
Chicago. He had built a thriving trading post there,
which included a large house, barns, stables, mills,
shops, livestock, and fine furniture.

De Sable's family, most certainly, had a comfortable
home in Chicago.

The house was located on a slope on the north side
of the Chicago River. A large porch on the front of the
house faced the river. The family must have enjoyed
many pleasant times sitting near the fieldstone fireplace
that was in the main room. The bill of sale of 1800
shows that the wooden house measured 40'×22'.

Actually the record of de Sable's sale to Lalime in
1800 is of the greatest importance. For the title of
founder of Chicago was not given to de Sable until more
than a hundred years later. During that time the founder
of Chicago was thought to be John H. Kinzie, a white
man who became a resident in 1804 and took over the
trading post from Jean Lalime.

Then, in the mid-1920s, the historian Milo M. Quaife
unearthed a document in French in the official records
at the Wayne County building in Detroit. This was
where the 1800 sale was recorded.

The marginal entry at the beginning of the document
states: "Inventory and Sale of Property Sold by Point
Sable to Jean Lalime." The document then begins: "In-

ventory taken and made before witnesses of the buildings, animals, etc., belonging to J. Bte. Point Sable at Chicago, the 7th May, 1800."

After a long listing of the items being sold, the document continues:

"I Jean Baptiste Point Sable by these presents certify to have sold by my own free will and consent all my property belonging to me at Chicago, I further oblige myself to deliver to Mr. Jean Lalime or his representatives all the articles above mentioned . . . for the sum of 6,000 livres of twenty coppers . . ."

After further arrangements about payments and transfers, the document concludes:

"Given under my hand and seal this 17th May, 1800, at St. Joseph, in the presence of witnesses undersigned after reading." The two witnesses to Lalime and de Sable's signatures were John Kinzie and William Burnet, St. Joseph traders.

The final notation on the sale transaction shows John Kinzie, a magistrate of peace in Wayne County, brought the deed to Josephy Voyez, J.P.W.C., and swore that he had seen it signed, sealed, and delivered, whereupon Voyez subscribed his name, recording the deed at Detroit on September 18, 1800.

Kinzie moved to Chicago in 1804, but can no longer be called the founder.

As Kinzie's daughter-in-law, Juliette, reports in her book *Wau-Bun*, "In giving the early history of Chicago the Indians say, with great simplicity, 'the first white man who settled here was a Negro.'"

After selling out in Chicago, de Sable seems to have spent a few years in Peoria. He then moved to St.

Charles, Missouri, where he spent the rest of his days.

Quaife says of de Sable: "He was enterprising and industrious, he inspired friendships which were not shaken by fortune's frown, and he commanded the confidence of men in responsible governmental and commercial stations. He was a true pioneer of civilization, leader of the unending procession of Chicago's swarming millions."

CHAPTER 3

SHE SANG OF COLUMBIA
Phillis Wheatley

A frail girl sat at a small oval table, deep in thought. She held a quilled pen in her thin hand. Phillis Wheatley glanced down at the paper and read out loud the title of her new poem, "His Excellency General Washington."

Just a few weeks ago, her master, Mr. John Wheatley, had told her the good news. On June 15, 1775, George Washington had been made Commander-in-Chief of the Revolutionary forces. His headquarters were in Cambridge, a few miles from Boston where she lived with the Wheatley family in a big house on King Street.

Phillis, a loyal patriot, was delighted with Washington's appointment. At last the American colonists had a strong leader to guide them in the war against the British.

She felt intensely about this struggle for freedom and independence. Seven years before, in 1769, after the Stamp Act was repealed, she had written a poem to King George III. The colonists had fought the act bitterly, and the little New England poet put her gratitude in verse.

Phyllis wanted this poem she was now working on to

Phillis Wheatley

be worthy of General Washington. So she chose her words carefully—glorious, poetic words in praise of this great American.

Outside she heard the servants talking as they performed the household tasks. But inside her room, it was quiet. Her heart, though, was beating loudly. She was finding it difficult to express her thoughts.

But she liked the first two lines of her poem to the General:

> Celestial choir! enthron'd in realms of light,
> *Columbia's* scenes of glorious toils I write.

She was the first to call America, her adopted country, by the name *Columbia*. She had taken this poetic name from Columbus, discoverer of the New World. Phillis dipped her pen in the pewter well of black ink and dotted the *i* in this new word.

For a long time she sat in a thoughtful pose, her chin on her hand. Occasionally she glanced at the fruitwood dresser. In the mirror she could see a tiny maid of twenty-two, with brown skin and dark eyes, dressed in a Puritan gray worsted gown with a wide white collar. She adjusted the perky little cap that covered her curly hair, the color of Africa's starless nights.

Once again she thought about General Washington. She admired him for his military record, but even more for his strength as a leader. She hoped that when the battles were won and there was peace, he would be the first king of this wonderful country.

So she wrote: First in peace and honours . . .

With these words this poem was to become important for another reason. Many consider this to be the first reference to Washington as "first in peace."

When Washington died in 1799, Resolutions presented to the House of Representatives, contained the following words:

"To the memory of the Man, first in war, first in peace, and first in the hearts of his countrymen."

This sentence, world famous since then, was undoubtedly inspired by Phillis Wheatley's poem.

By the autumn of 1775, the poem of forty-two lines was finished to the author's satisfaction. On October 26 of that year, while visiting in Providence, Rhode Island, she sent General Washington the following letter, written in the cramped script of the day:

Sir,

I have taken the freedom to address your Excellency in the enclosed poem, and entreat your acceptance, though I am not insensible of its inaccuracies.

Your being appointed by the Grand Continental Congress to be Generalissimo of the armies of North America, together with the fame of your virtues, excites sensations not easy to suppress. Your generosity, therefore, I presume, will pardon the attempt. Wishing your Excellency all possible success in the great cause you are so generously engaged in, I am

Your Excellency's most obedient humble servant,

Phillis Wheatley

General Washington did not reply to Phillis until February 28, 1776. On February 10, 1776, he com-

A page from the handwritten manuscript of Phillis Wheatley's first poem, "To the University of Cambridge, In New England, 1767." (Reproduced from the collections of the Library of Congress)

34

mented on the poem in a letter to Joseph Reed, explaining the delay. This is the last paragraph of a very long letter:

I recollect nothing else worth giving you the trouble of, unless you can be amused by reading a letter and poem addressed to me by Mrs. or Miss Phillis Wheatley. In searching over a parcel of papers the other day, in order to destroy such as were useless, I brought it to light again. At first, with a view of doing justice to her great poetical genius, I had a great mind to publish the poem; but not knowing whether it might not be considered rather as a mark of my own vanity, than as a compliment to her, I laid [it] aside, till I came across it again in the manner just mentioned.

Two weeks later, General Washington wrote to the poetess as follows:

Cambridge, February 28, 1776

Miss Phillis: Your favour of the 26th of October did not reach my hands 'till the middle of December. Time enough, you will say, to have given an answer ere this. Granted. But a variety of important occurrences, continually interposing to distract the mind and withdraw the attention, I hope will apologize for the delay, and plead my excuse for the seeming, but not real neglect.

I thank you most sincerely for your polite notice of me, in the elegant Lines you enclosed; and however undeserving I may be of such encomium and panegyrick, the style and manner exhibit a striking proof of your great poetical Talents. In honour of which, as a tribute justly due to you, I would have published the Poem, had I not been apprehensive, that, while I only meant to give the World this new instance of your genius, I might have incurred the imputation of Vanity. This and nothing else, determined me not to give it place in the public Prints.

If you should ever come to Cambridge, or near Head Quarters, I shall be happy to see a person so favoured by the Muses and to whom Nature has been so liberal and beneficent in her dispensations. I am, with great respect, your obedient, humble servant;

Geo. Washington

A few days before the British evacuated Boston, Phillis Wheatley visited Washington in Cambridge. She was with the Commander-in-Chief for about half an hour.

Her poem to Washington and his letter were published in the *Pennsylvania Magazine* for April 1776. Thomas Paine, the patriot, was the magazine's editor.

As a small child, Phillis was kidnaped by slavers and brought from Senegal, in West Africa, to America in a slave ship.

Almost nothing is known of her African childhood or background. W. A. Jackson says that she belonged "to the Kaffir race, a people characterized by intelligence, industry and uprightness." She was probably born in 1753.

Dr. G. Herbert Renfro points out the "only distinct

impression" Phillis brought from Africa "was that every morning her mother was accustomed to 'pour out water before the rising sun . . .'"

Jackson's Memoir describes the horrible experience on the ship that brought her to America:

"She was kidnapped and sold to the master of a slave ship bound for Boston. She was imprisoned on the middle deck of the ship, with about seventy-five other girls, in a room thirteen by twenty-five feet, and five feet eight inches high. The allotted space for each girl being four feet six inches by one foot. Her food consisted of rice, yams, and horse beans, twice a day, which diet was occasionally varied by boiled beef. She arrived in Boston weary and broken down from her long sea voyage . . . and was clothed only by a piece of soiled carpet about her waist, in which shameful condition she awaited the coming of a purchaser."

No slave has ever been more fortunate than this little girl was in getting so fine a master and mistress.

John Wheatley was a prosperous tailor-merchant of Boston. He and his wife, Susanna, had two children, Nathaniel and Mary, twins, then about eighteen. They had several old slaves in their household, but they needed someone younger who, when properly trained, could serve as Mrs. Wheatley's personal maid.

So one day in 1761 Mrs. Wheatley went on board the slave ship. Hundreds of black people were huddled in a small, poorly lighted, badly ventilated area.

But Mrs. Wheatley was drawn to one tragic little creature—a child with pathetic, beseeching dark eyes.

The Wheatleys paid "only a trifle" for the sickly little

girl. In fact the captain was anxious to sell her as soon as he could, for he feared she might die before he could find a purchaser for her.

The frightened child, who knew only the language spoken by her tribe in West Africa, was brought home to an elegant residence.

"This child will have to learn our language," Mrs. Wheatley told her husband, "before she can understand us."

"That may be difficult," Mr. Wheatley said, "but first she must have a name. What are you going to call her?"

"I think I'll call her Phillis," Mrs. Wheatley said.

"Then Phillis should be the first word she should learn," Mr. Wheatley said.

His wife nodded. "I will teach her her name today."

Later that day, the plump middle-aged woman and the delicate child sat on a bench in the Wheatley garden. The frail little girl, now in a long gray dress, sat primly beside her. Her dark skin shone, for she had just been bathed. Big eyes in a thin face looked up at the motherly woman.

"Your name is Phillis," Mrs. Wheatley said slowly and distinctly, gently touching her on the shoulder.

The child's eyes never left her mistress.

"Phillis," Mrs. Wheatley smiled, as once again she touched the Negro girl's shoulder. "Phillis means a green branch of a tree, like that one," she said, pointing to a sapling by the bench. "You remind us of a tiny little tree," the woman said. Warmth and love were in her soft voice. "A tree that needs good food, bright sunshine, and tender care." She touched the girl's tightly curled hair. Again she repeated, "Your name is Phillis."

"Your name is Phillis," Mrs. Wheatley said slowly and distinctly.

The child looked up at her questioningly.

"Phillis. Phillis." Again Mrs. Wheatley touched the child's thin shoulder. "Phillis is your name. Phillis."

"Phillis?" the little girl finally said, as she touched her own shoulder.

Mrs. Wheatley nodded. "Phillis."

The slave girl proved to be bright, alert, and eager to learn. Mary, some ten years older than Phillis, took special pleasure in teaching her. Phillis came to be accepted as a member of the family.

She wrote to her friend, Obour Tanner, on March 21, 1774, shortly after Mrs. Wheatley died:

> I was a poor little outcast and a stranger when she took me in; not only into her house, but I presently became a sharer in her most tender affections. I was treated by her more like her child than her servant; . . .

Phillis, although a slave, had no hard duties. Renfro quotes a memoir written later by a member of the family:

"Mrs. Wheatley did not require or permit her services as a domestic, but she would sometimes allow her to polish a table or dust an apartment, or engage in some other trifling occupation that would break in upon her sedentary habits . . ."

The same relative also wrote: "Phillis ate of her bread and was to her as a daughter, for she returned her affection with unbounded gratitude, and was so devoted to her interests as to have no will in opposition to that of her benefactress."

Treated in this manner, Phillis blossomed into a

lovely woman with much charm. Had she been purchased by a harsh slaveowner, she probably would
never have developed into a poet. As a favored slave of
gentle people she eventually took the family name,
publishing poems and signing letters as Phillis Wheatley. However, as late as 1771, a record refers to her
merely as "Phillis, the servant of Mr. Wheatley." Despite preferential treatment, she remained a slave for a
dozen or more years. She was set free informally by
Mary in 1778, after Mr. Wheatley died. At that time
Phillis was about twenty-five years old.

Even though she was a slave for a long time, Phillis
was grateful for the Wheatleys' kind treatment, and
never regretted being brought from Africa to this country. She expressed this sentiment often. In a letter she
wrote on May 19, 1772, to Obour Tanner, she stresses
this. Tanner was an educated slave of Newport, Rhode
Island, who may have come from Africa on the same
ship with Phillis.

> . . . let us rejoice in and adore the wonders of
> God's infinite Love in bringing us from a land sem-
> blant of darkness itself, and where the divine light
> of revelation [being obscured] is in darkness. Here the
> knowledge of the true God and eternal life are made
> manifest; but there profound ignorance overshadows
> the land.

She expressed similar feelings in an earlier poem in
1767, which said in part:

'Twas not long since I left my native shore
The land of errors, and Egyptian gloom:

Father of mercy, 'twas thy gracious hand
Brought me in safety from those dark abodes.

The whole Wheatley family marveled at Phillis' excellent mind and the fact that she seemed to learn everything so quickly. Mary, who enjoyed teaching Phillis, never ceased to be amazed.

"She's like deep rich soil that drinks water thirstily," Mary told her mother. "She is thirsty for education."

Phillis seemed to have the kind of mind that could absorb a great deal of knowledge. She studied the Bible, classical mythology, Greek and Roman writers, and eighteenth-century English poetry. Her favorite poet was Alexander Pope, whose style influenced her own.

Her remarkable progress in her studies in a new language is described in a letter Mr. Wheatley sent to her publishers. Probably the firm had asked Mr. Wheatley to vouch that his slave had written the poems. This letter was included in her book of poems in 1773.

Phillis was brought from *Africa* to *America*, in the year 1761, between seven and eight Years of age, without any assistance from School Education, and by only what she was taught in the Family, she in sixteen Months' Time from her arrival, attained the English Language, to which she was an utter Stranger before; to such a Degree, as to read any, the most difficult parts of the Sacred Writings, to the great Astonishment of all who heard her.

As to her writing, her own Curiosity led her to it; and this she learned in so short a Time, that in the year 1765, she wrote a letter to the Rev. Mr. Occom, the *Indian* Minister, while in England.

She had a great Inclination to learn the Latin Tongue, and she has made some Progress in it. This Relation is given by her Master, who bought her, and with whom she now lives.

John Wheatley

Boston, November 14, 1772.

The Wheatleys gave Phillis treatment not usually accorded a slave. She was permitted to have light and heat in her room so that she could get up at any hour and write. She was also permitted to join the Old South Church in Boston. She became a communicant August 18, 1771. She had been christened or baptized three years before by the Reverend Sewell.

When Mary Wheatley married Reverend John Lathrop on January 31, 1771, and left her parents' home, Phillis was very sad. Mary and Phillis had become good friends.

Through the years the Wheatleys never ceased to marvel at Phillis' talents and ability. More and more of Boston's important citizens learned of her when they visited the Wheatley mansion.

Phillis started writing poetry while still in her teens. Her first poem was written in 1767. She called it "To the University of Cambridge, In New England, 1767."

The first lines read:

While an intrinsic ardor prompts to write
The muses promise to assist my pen.

The first of her poems to be published was printed in a pamphlet in 1770. "An Elegiac Poem on the Death of George Whitefield" was probably her most frequently published work. One writer has reported that this poem appeared "in at least six different editions, in Boston, Philadelphia, and New York, within a few months." All told, it was published at least eight times separately, as well as appearing in the 1773 book and its numerous subsequent editions. This well-known poem praised the famed English preacher, George Whitefield.

Phillis became a celebrity with the publication of this poem. Now word spread among the intellectuals throughout the nation that there was a fine young Negro poet who lived in Boston. Her fame next spread to England and the Continent.

Phillis Wheatley had always been delicate and frail. Probably she was sensitive to the cold, snowy winters of New England. Then in the early 1770s her health began to fail. The Wheatleys' family physician advised a change of climate, possibly a trip abroad. Nathaniel Wheatley was planning a business trip to England, so Phillis went with him.

Before she sailed across the Atlantic Ocean, she wrote a thirteen-stanza poem, "A Farewell to America," May 7, 1773. She dedicated it "To Mrs. S. W." The initials stand for her beloved mistress, Susanna Wheatley.

The third stanza tells how difficult this parting would be for her and her mistress.

> Susannah mourns, nor can I bear,
> to see the Crystal show'r,

Or mark the tender falling tear
At sad departure's hour . . .

In England, she spent a great deal of time with Se-
lina Shirley, the Countess of Huntingdon, with whom
she had corresponded. This woman was the daughter
of the Earl of Ferrer and the widow of the Earl of
Huntingdon. She was a patron of the Reverend George
Whitefield, and became the sole trustee of his institutions in Georgia when he died. Phillis wrote an elegy at
the time of Whitefield's death and in it mentioned the
Countess:

Great Countess, we Americans revere
Thy name, and mingle in thy grief sincere

The Countess introduced Phillis to fashionable British society. She had planned to present her to King
George III at court, but Phillis sailed back to America
before she had the chance to meet the monarch she had
once written about in a poem. Her mistress was ill and
Phillis longed to be with her.

In a letter she wrote to Obour Tanner, October 30,
1773, after she had returned to Boston, she told of her
English experience:

"The friends I found there among the nobility and
gentry, their benevolent conduct towards me, the unex-
pected and unmerited civility and complaisance with
which I was treated by all, fill me with astonishment.
I can scarcely realize it." She also mentioned to her
African friend that the trip had not "conduced to the
recovery (in a great measure) of my health."

But because of her friends in London, her only book

The Countess of Huntingdon introduced Phillis to fashionable British society.

was published. It may even have appeared in print before she left England.

Poems on Various Subjects, Religious and Moral (London: Bell, 1773), had a portrait of the poet, and was dedicated to the Countess of Huntingdon. It contained thirty-eight of her poems. There were fourteen elegies, six occasional, two paraphrasing the Bible, sixteen representing her best productions by the time she was twenty.

The publisher's preface to the original 1773 edition read in part:

"The following Poems were written originally for the Amusement of the Author, as they were the Products of her leisure moments. She had no Intention ever to have published them; nor would they now have made their Appearance, but at the Importunity of many of her best and most generous Friends, to whom she considers herself, as under the greatest Obligations.

"As her attempts in Poetry are now sent into the world, it is hoped the Critic will not severely censure their Defects; and we presume they have too much Merit to be cast aside with Contempt, as worthless and trifling Effusions."

Eighteen prominent citizens attested to the fact that Phillis Wheatley was qualified to write the poems. Some of these people included Governor Thomas Hutchinson, John Hancock, and Reverend Samuel Mather.

With the publication of her book in 1773, and of her poem and letter to Washington in 1776, Phillis was at the height of her success. Then trouble began piling up on her frail shoulders. Four years after Mrs. Wheatley's death, her husband died.

After Nathaniel Wheatley went to England to live, Phillis was left alone. She married John Peters, a free Negro like herself, in April 1778. There are many conflicting reports about her husband. One person has written that he "kept a shop, wore a wig, carried a cane, and felt himself superior to all kinds of labor." Another writer has mentioned that he was "a grocer, barber, baker, lawyer, or doctor." Even with all these talents, Peters had difficulty providing a living for his family.

So Phillis, in 1779, tried to raise money by publishing a second volume of poems. An advertisement ran in the *Boston Evening Post and General Advertiser* of October 30, 1779, seeking subscribers. The book was to consist of thirty-three poems and thirteen letters. Only two poems are in existence: "His Excellency Gen. Washington" and "On the Capture of Gen. Lee."

The ad had said that the work would be printed as soon as enough persons ordered it. Unfortunately, there were not enough people interested and the book did not appear.

Phillis was terribly disappointed, for her family needed money. These were hard times. She and her husband lived in poverty at one time in Wilmington, Massachusetts. For a while she stayed in Boston with a niece of Mrs. Wheatley. At another time, she and her husband lived on Queen Street in Boston. They had three children, but the first two died in the early 1780s.

Phillis worked in a cheap lodging house to support her family, but she was not accustomed to such long, hard, trying work. Her husband was put in prison for debt. In the meantime, Nathaniel Wheatley died in England in the summer of 1783. As his twin sister Mary had died some years before, this was Phillis' last link to influential white people, and her pride seems to have kept her from appealing to others.

Phillis died on December 5, 1784. She was thirty-one. Her third child, still a baby, died a few hours after its mother.

Phillis Wheatley was probably the best known of all American Negroes of her day. Her book of poems was printed in many editions and widely read.

Much of the interest in her was due to curiosity over a Negro being able to write poetry. But she was often cited by such people as the great English abolitionist, Thomas Clarkson, as proof of what Negroes are capable of. She was a strong argument for the case against slavery.

Phillis Wheatley was undoubtedly the pre-eminent American Negro poet until the time of the much greater Paul Laurence Dunbar. Other Negro poets of her generation included Lucy Terry Prince, Jupiter Hammond, and George Moses Horton.

Especially striking in her poetry is her seeming lack of race consciousness. Except for the autobiographical lines in the poems to Lord Dartmouth and to the University of Cambridge students, and except for the short poem "On Being Brought from Africa to America," one could hardly tell that she was a slave from Africa.

Jupiter Hammond wrote a tribute to her, but she did not write tributes to any of her fellow Negroes, such as

Crispus Attucks (hero of the Boston Massacre), Peter Salem (Bunker Hill hero), shipowner Paul Cuffe, or scientist Benjamin Banneker. Her only exception was her poem, "To S.M., A Young African Painter, On Seeing His Works," addressed to Scipio Moorhead. But the poem showed no race consciousness other than the title.

Her poem to Washington remains one of the first, if not the first, to salute him in poetry, a fitting tribute to the Father of our Country:

> Proceed, great chief, with virtue on thy side,
> Thy ev'ry action let the goddess guide.
> A crown, a mansion, and a throne that shine,
> With gold unfading, Washington! be thine.

CHAPTER 4

HE REACHED FOR
THE STARS

Benjamin Banneker

Young Benjamin Banneker sat on the doorstep of his grandmother's house in Maryland, looking at the night sky with all its stars. His grandmother sat beside him. Suddenly a sparkling white object shot across the heavens. Seconds later it disappeared.

"Where did it go?" he asked, puzzled. The boy leaned his head back as far as he could, searching eagerly for the mysterious star. But his sharp black eyes could not find it.

"Grandma, where *did* the star go?" he asked. Benjamin often asked his grandmother questions about things he did not understand.

"I do not know," she answered, shaking her head. Her straight brown hair, streaked with white, was drawn severely back from a fair face. "Maybe the Book can tell us," she added, as she got up from the wooden step.

Together they went inside the weather-beaten cabin. His grandmother lighted a candle, and Benjamin,

Benjamin Banneker

standing on his bare toes, reached for the Bible on the shelf. He carried the heavy book to the crudely hewn table.

Mrs. Banneker had taught Benjamin his letters. On Sunday mornings Benjamin used to read the Bible to her. She hoped he would grow up to be a religious man.

His grandmother, who had learned to read as a girl growing up in England, turned the pages and searched for passages about the stars and the heavens. But she could not find the answer about the shooting star.

"You are a bright boy and you can read," she said proudly. "Someday you will find the answer," she prophesied, "then you can explain why a star falls."

"I will find the answer," Benjamin said, looking out the doorway at the mysterious black sky. There was a look of determination in his eyes.

Benjamin's grandmother had taught him many wonderful things about nature. He knew where to find roots, grasses, fruits, nuts, and gay-colored berries that were good to eat. His sensitive nose quivered like a rabbit's at sounds and smells. He knew when the howling wind changed its course. He knew when a deer or fox had been in their fields or orchards. He knew how to tell the age of a tree.

But he could not understand what had happened to the star, and why his grandmother could not tell him. It remained a puzzle to bother him for a long time.

When Benjamin Banneker was growing up, Maryland was a colony belonging to England. Benjamin was born on November 9, 1731, three and one-half months before George Washington. His birthplace was his grandparents' farm near the Patapsco River, about ten miles from Baltimore.

Benjamin was born free. His mother's mother, Mollie Welsh, had been deported from England in the late seventeenth century as punishment for a minor offense that was not her fault. She had been convicted of stealing a pail of milk, when in reality a cow had kicked it over. This innocent young woman worked for seven years for a tobacco planter to pay her debt for her passage across the Atlantic.

Mollie had saved a little money. By the end of her long term of service, she already knew what she would do with the coins that were safely hidden away. She bought land by a spring in the Patapsco River Valley in Maryland.

After struggling alone for a short period, Mollie Welsh realized she could not farm without help. So one day, in 1692, she walked the ten long miles to Chesapeake Bay where a slave ship was anchored. She bought two African slaves, who helped her on the farm. One of them, named Bannaky, claimed to be the son of an African king. He had great dignity, good manners, and was strong and powerful. He was also highly intelligent. Mollie Welsh later gave both Africans their freedom and afterward married Bannaky, whose name later became Banneker. Their oldest child was Mary. When she grew up, Mary married Robert, formerly a slave from Africa, who worked on a plantation nearby. Robert had no family name, so he took his wife's last name, Banneker. He was thrifty and industrious. Benjamin was their oldest child and only son. He had three sisters, Mollie, Minta, and Tillie.

One brisk spring morning in 1737, six-year-old Benjamin woke up and scrambled into his clothes. All he could think of was "This is the day!" Today his parents and his grandparents were going to deliver several thousand pounds of fine tobacco to Richard Gist. The tobacco had been grown on his grandparents' farm.

At the breakfast table, the family was unusually quiet. Benjamin was bursting with eagerness. He couldn't sit quietly in his chair and eat. Finally he said, "This *is* the day, Mama, isn't it?"

She smiled and said, "Yes, Benjamin, this is the day!"

His parents, Robert and Mary Banneker, had waited many years for this chance. Now, with the earnings from the tobacco, they were going to buy land. They were well aware that they were assuming a big responsibility. It would mean putting in longer hours each day than they were now doing. But both were hard workers and liked to be outdoors, and their children were old enough to help them.

There were few free Negroes at that time in Maryland who owned large farms. But the younger Bannekers were eager to own their own property. The grandparents had done well, and they also hoped to succeed.

The purchase of this land proved to be a good investment. People often talked about the fine crops this Negro family produced, even when there was no rain and other farmers had poor crops.

Benjamin's father had grown crops in Africa and perhaps felt closer to the soil than his neighbors. So he had dug ditches. Then when the soil was dry, the water from the deep springs located on the hill irrigated the parched land. He and his wife Mary had also built gates and locks to control the flow of the spring water. These same springs, known as the Bannaky springs, also supplied water to the land owned by Benjamin's grandparents.

Benjamin also started to school that year. He could hardly wait for the Monday morning in September. At last he would have many books to read. Then, too, he had so many questions he wanted to ask. If the teacher didn't know all the answers, then he surely could find them in the books.

"You will like school," his grandmother told him. "Mind what your teacher tells you and be respectful." She patted his curly head. "Soon you will be at the head of your class."

"I'll try, Grandma," Benjamin said, as he started out the door.

The school was a short way from the farm, and Benjamin ran all the way, clutching the slate in his hand. But when he reached the schoolhouse, he straightened his tie and brushed his white shirt and walked slowly up the steps. The Quaker schoolmaster was at the desk talking to several white and colored children.

Until he was sent to school, Benjamin had had little contact with white people, except his Grandmother Banneker whom he loved very much. The only book Benjamin knew was the large Bible he read at her house.

But now that he was going to school, he was fascinated by the books his teacher showed him.

Every school day was a new adventure for Benjamin. He listened carefully to every word the teacher said.

Benjamin repeated the words to himself, so that his way of saying them would be the way his teacher spoke.

But it was arithmetic that he liked best of all. He quickly learned how to add and subtract, and he liked multiplication and division.

The first time the teacher gave the students problems to solve, Benjamin had the answers in no time at all. He raised his hand to let the teacher know that he was finished with his work.

"Have you worked all the problems?" the teacher asked, as he peered over his eyeglasses.

"Yes, sir," Benjamin answered.

"Have you checked them? You know you must prove them."

Benjamin nodded.

"Bring your slate to my desk," the teacher said.

Benjamin walked proudly to the front of the room and placed the slate on the big oak desk.

"The answers are correct," the teacher said a few minutes later. "I shall have to assign you much more difficult problems."

In 1746, when he was fifteen, and his nine years of schooling were over, Benjamin was only as far as "double position" in arithmetic.

Jacob Hall, an old servant of the Hall family of Baltimore County, proudly told some people: "When all the rest of the boys played outdoors and were seeking amusement, Benjamin's only delight was to dive into his books."

Benjamin missed going to school, especially because there were so few books at home. He continued to be a

"The answers are correct," the teacher said. "I shall have to assign you much more difficult problems."

careful observer of nature and listened intently to anyone who could give him information. Mr. J. H. B. Latrobe, speaking before the Maryland Historical Society in 1845, said that Banneker "became gradually possessed of a fund of general knowledge which it was difficult to find even among those who were far more favored by opportunity than he was."

As a young man, Benjamin Banneker did not seem to have any desire to leave his family or the farm. He seemed to prefer to remain at home, for there was a close family tie.

His parents' farm was one of the best kept in that part of Maryland. The Bannekers had fine horses and cows, healthy fruit trees, and many hives of bees.

Benjamin was twenty-eight when his father died. Seventy-two acres of farmland were left to the only son, Benjamin, and his mother, as joint heirs. The remainder was left to Benjamin's three sisters.

Since Benjamin had worked with his father, he was able to continue living comfortably from the produce grown on the farm, including the fruit, vegetables, and honey from the apiary. His mother, Mary, who like his grandmother knew about the herbs that grew wild in that section, did most of the selling of the farm products.

Benjamin plowed and hoed the fields, planted crops and cared for the bees, but he also found time to study mathematics.

People who knew Benjamin Banneker were impressed with his ability. They often commented on his keen mind, and the ease with which he solved difficult mathematical problems. When, in 1761, he built a wooden clock, his fame spread far beyond Baltimore County. At that time Benjamin was thirty years old.

Banneker had never seen a clock, but he had seen a pocket watch which served as his model. Probably there was not a clock within fifty miles of the farm. He worked a long time on the clock. He had few of the right tools that would have made the work easier, but he did have the watch which he took apart. The clock he made was many times larger than the watch.

A century later, an article in *The Atlantic Monthly* described the wooden clock:

". . . this was the first clock of which every portion was made in America. It is certain that it was as purely his own invention as if none had ever been made before."

When word got around that a comparatively uneducated Negro had made a clock with wooden parts that worked, visitors came for miles around to the Banneker farm.

One person declared that the clock was "perfect in every detail, for years it struck the hours with faultless precision, and was considered a mechanical masterpiece by all who saw it."

As the days went by, people became more aware of Banneker's remarkable memory, his mathematical ability, and his excellent English. He was now recognized as one of the best mathematicians in that area, for he was astonishingly rapid in solving problems. Scholars from other sections of the thirteen colonies sent him puzzles to test him. As soon as he received them, he would sit down at his table in his scantily furnished

Benjamin patterned his wooden clock on a pocket watch. It was the first clock whose parts were made entirely in America.

house and start figuring them out. With his quick mind, he would have the correct answers in no time at all.

Banneker found that he much preferred solving and making up problems to working on the farm. But his livelihood was the farm. In order to have food, he had to plant crops and hoe the fields. But this was not as exciting as working out a problem.

Finally he got tenants for most of the farm, keeping a small portion for himself. But they wouldn't pay him, and they stole his fruit and goods.

Actually his responsibilities for the family farm troubled him a great deal. He had fine orchards that produced sweet juicy pears and cherries. The boys in the neighborhood also knew about the Banneker orchards. They would knock at his door and ask permission to pick some of his fruit.

The kind Negro, whose hair was now turning white, would agree. Then, after he closed his door and went back to his studies, the boys would take most of his fruit, sometimes even before it was ripe. Even when he talked to them, and offered them half of his fruit, it made no difference.

Most of the time he was not disturbed with the petty jealousies and temper of the people with whom he frequently had to deal. On a page in one of his *Almanacs*, printed years later, appears this comment:

"Evil communications corrupt good manners. I hope to live to hear that good communications correct bad manners."

Even though Banneker was receiving recognition, he was actually very lonely. He had never married, so he did not have a wife or children to talk to. There was no one in his neighborhood who could discuss mathematical and scientific problems with him.

Then something wonderful happened.

In 1772 Banneker was forty-one. That year the three Ellicott brothers—John, Joseph, and Andrew—moved to Patapsco Valley. They were millers. Their father, Andrew, an English Quaker, had migrated to Bucks County, Pennsylvania, about 1730. Joseph, like Banneker, had made a clock that had received considerable attention.

The Ellicotts became lifelong friends of Banneker and helped him in many ways. Indeed, their arrival marked the turning point in his career.

While the Ellicott mills were being built and the machinery brought from Pennsylvania, the Ellicotts bought provisions for their workmen from the Banneker farm. Banneker's mother always selected for them the largest and freshest vegetables and fruits, the fattest chickens and the best grade of honey. She packed them carefully and walked to the mills which were several miles away. This she did almost daily.

Although most farmers in that part of Maryland grew tobacco, the Ellicott brothers encouraged the farmers to grow wheat. They claimed that there was a bigger market for grain. The Ellicott flour mills thrived. A prosperous community, called Ellicott Mills, developed. It was chartered in 1775.

What interested Banneker most about the mills was the machinery that ground the wheat into flour. He studied the big rollers, fascinated. The Ellicotts were impressed with this fine man who came often to the mills. They entertained him in their home and visited him at his farm. The Ellicotts were also mechanically and scientifically inclined. George Ellicott became Banneker's closest friend.

One day, in 1787, when Banneker was visiting at his friend's home, George Ellicott offered to lend him some books on astronomy.

Banneker was delighted. When he was ready to return to his farm with the books, George Ellicott said, "I'll be over soon to help you with the tables and instruments."

"I shall appreciate that very much," Banneker said.

But George Ellicott was called away unexpectedly on business. When he returned, he went over to see Banneker, expecting to explain certain principles. To his amazement, he found that Banneker had already mastered them and was absorbed in studying them. At this time Banneker was about fifty-six years old.

James McHenry of Baltimore wrote a memoir of Banneker, dated April 21, 1791, for publication in Banneker's first *Almanac*. In this memoir, McHenry stated:

"It is about three years since Mr. George Ellicott lent his Mayer's Tables, Ferguson's Astronomy, Leadbetter's Lunar Tables and some astronomic instruments, but without accompanying them with either hint or instruction, that might further his studies or lead him to apply them to any useful result. These books and instruments, the first of the kind he had ever seen, opened a new world to Benjamin, and from thence forward he employed his leisure in astronomical researches."

From that time on, astronomy became almost an obsession with Benjamin Banneker. As a boy, he had been fascinated with the stars that shone so brightly, but up to now he had never had the good fortune to see books on the subject.

The last twenty years of his life, Banneker devoted most of his time to scientific studies.

At first the farm was a big problem. What could he do? What plan could he work out so that he would not only have a small income for the rest of his life, but his farm would continue to produce good crops.

In 1783 he talked the problem over with George Ellicott. His good friend listened carefully to the points that Banneker brought up. Finally Banneker suggested a plan.

"I believe I shall live fifteen years," Benjamin Banneker said, "and I consider my land worth 180 pounds Maryland currency. By receiving 12 pounds a year for fifteen years, I shall in the contemplated time receive its full value. If, on the contrary, I shall die before that day, you will be at liberty to take possession."

His good friend agreed to this, for he knew how much it meant to Banneker.

In estimating the number of years he would live, Banneker guessed wrong. Some have said that this is the only calculation he was ever mistaken about! Banneker lived eight years longer than the fifteen he calculated.

His loyal friend, however, continued to pay the yearly amount of money to Banneker over his objections.

"The land has increased in value during this period," George Ellicott assured Banneker.

At long last this weighty problem about his farm was

solved. He could now study as many hours each day as he desired. It was a great relief to him not to have to worry about the farm.

Every night as soon as it was dark, Banneker would leave his log cabin. A blanket over his arm, he would walk over to a certain tree. He carefully spread the blanket on the ground, and then he made himself comfortable on his back, so that he could watch the stars. Until they disappeared in the early dawn, Banneker was still there, his hands under his head, his black eyes concentrating on the heavens. As one writer has said:

"His favorite time for study was night, when he could look out on the planets, whose story he was reading, and whose laws he was gradually but surely watching."

As soon as the sun rose, reluctantly, he got up, stretched, and went inside his house to sleep.

His neighbors, who did not understand Banneker's peculiar habits, shook their heads.

"He is a lazy old man," they said. "When he was young he was a hard worker and was proud of his fine crops."

What his neighbors said about him did not seem to bother Banneker. He was too busy with his scientific observations. Through his study of astronomy, Banneker predicted a solar eclipse in 1789.

Because of his mathematical training, he detected errors in the learned treatises of Ferguson and Leadbetter from which he had first learned astonomy.

Banneker also was keenly aware of nature. Observations he made in his manuscript memoranda of material for possible use in his *Almanacs* show this.

He noted that locusts seem to recur in seventeen-year cycles, and then explained how they lay eggs.

He observed that a stronger hive of bees seemed to have taken the honey of a weaker hive and killed the bees when they tried to recover their honey.

On August 27, 1797, he wrote the following: "Standing at my door I heard the discharge of a gun, and in four or five seconds after the discharge, the small shot came rattling around me, one or two of which struck the house; which plainly demonstrates that the velocity of sound is greater than that of a cannon bullet."

Until the 1790s, Banneker's fame was still essentially local. Then in the next decade he received national and world recognition in two ways.

The Congress of the United States, in July 1790, passed a law to establish a permanent capital on the Potomac River. The President, George Washington, was authorized to pick the site, to name the three commissioners to survey and plan the location of the buildings.

Seven months later, in February 1791, President Washington sent Andrew Ellicott III to survey the general site, under the direction of the three commissioners. The actual plan for the city was to be made by the Frenchman, Pierre Charles L'Enfant.

At the request of Mr. Ellicott and Thomas Jefferson, then Secretary of State, Benjamin Banneker was appointed to assist Ellicott in surveying the land. This was the first presidential appointment of a Negro and the first national recognition of Banneker's abilities.

The Georgetown *Weekly Ledger* of March 12, 1791, mentioned the coming of Ellicott and L'Enfant, "attended by Benjamin Banneker, an Ethiopian whose

Benjamin Banneker, as the first Negro appointee of a President, worked on the survey of Washington, D.C., with George Ellicott.

abilities as surveyor and astronomer already proves that Mr. Jefferson's concluding that race of men void of mental endowments was without foundation."

The commissioners were impressed with this distinguished Negro. His suit was of fine broadcloth, made in the old style of a plain coat, with straight collar and long waistcoat. He wore a broad-brimmed hat.

It is believed that Banneker had learned surveying from the Ellicotts. He worked ably on the survey, impressing his colleagues. He served from 1791 to 1793. The commissioners invited him to have meals with them in the headquarters, but he did not accept. Instead he ate at a separate table but in the same room.

L'Enfant, who was extremely temperamental, got into a dispute with the commissioners and left. Ellicott, probably assisted by Banneker, reproduced from memory the plan that L'Enfant refused to turn over on leaving. In 1792 Andrew Ellicott III became the first Surveyor-General of the United States.

George Ellicott encouraged Banneker to compile some of his mathematical and astronomical calculations into an almanac. This was to be Banneker's second widely-known accomplishment. Almanacs then were one of the highest examples of scientific achievement. They were popular and served as an essential source for weather and tide news and entertainment.

While helping to lay out the nation's capital, Banneker worked on his *Almanac*. He finished the manuscript during the summer of 1791.

The Ellicotts got James McHenry of Baltimore interested in Banneker's project. McHenry, a Maryland state senator, was later John Adams' Secretary of War. With

McHenry's aid, Goddard and Angell, Baltimore publishers, brought out Banneker's first *Almanac* for 1792.

The publishers proudly proclaimed that they were gratified "in the opportunity of presenting . . . what must be considered an extraordinary effect of genius . . . a complete and accurate Ephemeris for the year 1792, calculated by a sable descendent of Africa, who by this specimen of ingenuity envices to demonstrate that mental powers and endowments are not exclusive excellence of white people, but that the rays of science may alike illume the minds of men of every clime, however they may differ in the color of their skin . . ."

Banneker was sixty years old when his first *Almanac* was published. It undoubtedly helped to change the prevailing image of the Negro. Banneker continued to publish *Almanacs* regularly until 1802.

In his *Almanac* for 1793, Banneker proposed a remarkable Plan for Peace. He suggested that a Secretary of Peace be appointed to the President's cabinet. While much of this Peace Plan was impractical, it did contain farsighted demands for free universal schooling, abolition of capital punishment, and disarmament. The plan, too, was a great tribute to Banneker's independent thinking.

Banneker sent Secretary of State Thomas Jefferson a manuscript copy of his first *Almanac*, along with a letter dated August 19, 1791, protesting Jefferson's prejudice against the Negro. Banneker had once written about his people: "We are a race of beings who have long labored under the abuse and censure of the world." He was therefore sensitive to the opinions of prominent people about his race.

BANNEKER's

ALMANACK,

AND

EPHEMERIS

FOR THE

YEAR OF OUR LORD 1793;

BEING

THE FIRST AFTER BISSEXTILE OR LEAP-YEAR:

CONTAINING

THE MOTIONS OF THE SUN AND
MOON;

THE TRUE PLACES AND ASPECTS
OF THE PLANETS;

THE RISING AND SETTING OF
THE SUN;

RISING, SETTING, AND SOUTHING
OF THE MOON;

THE LUNATIONS, CONJUNCTIONS,
AND ECLIPSES;

AND

THE RISING, SETTING, AND SOUTHING OF THE
PLANETS AND NOTED FIXED STARS.

PHILADELPHIA:

PRINTED AND SOLD BY *JOSEPH CRUKSHANK*, NO. 87, HIGH-
STREET.

The title page of one of Benjamin Banneker's early almanacs. (From
the Schomburg Collection)

APRIL, Fourth Month, *hath* 30 *Days.*

	D.	H.	M.	
Laſt ☾	3	4	48	A.
New ●	10	11	26	M.
Firſt ☽	18	0	0	M.
Full ○	26	0	9	M.

☊				
	1		14	Deg.
	11	♍	13	Deg.
	21		13	Deg.

Planets' Places, &c.

Days	☉	♄	♃	♂	♀	☿	☽'s Lat.
	♈	♉	♐	♈	♉	♉	
1	12	2	2	22	27	0	5 N.
7	18	2	1	26	♊ 2	8	0 N.
13	24	3	1	♉ 1	6	10	5 S.
19	♉ 0	4	0	5	10	10	2 S.
25	6	5	0	10	13	6	4 N.

		Remarkable days, &c.	☉ ri.	☉ ſet	☽ pl.	☽ riſe	☽ ſou.
1	2	Day 12 32	5 44	6 16	♐ 13	11 37	3 50
2	3	*Clear and pleaſant :*	5 43	6 17	27	morn.	4 47
3	4	Pleiades ſet 10 7	5 41	6 19	♑ 11	0 39	5 46
4	5	St. Ambroſe.	5 40	6 20	26	1 37	6 44
5	6	*cloudy and*	5 39	6 21	♒ 11	2 32	7 46
6	7	Days increaſe 3 28	5 38	6 22	26	3 24	8 42
7	F	♀ greateſt elongation.	5 36	6 24	♓ 11	4 4	9 36
8	2	*like for rain :*	5 35	6 25	25	4 43	10 32
9	3	Regulus ſouth 8 43	5 34	6 26	♈ 9	5 20	11 23
10	4	*clear and cold :*	5 33	6 27	23	ſets	aſt. 14
11	5	Spica ♍ ſouth 11 55	5 32	6 28	♉ 7	7 49	1 2
12	6	*but ſoon*	5 30	6 30	20	8 52	1 54
13	7	Eagle riſes 11 43	5 29	6 31	♊ 3	9 53	2 43
14	F	Day 13 4	5 28	6 32	16	10 50	3 33
15	2	*changes to*	5 27	6 33	28	11 41	4 24
16	3	♃ ſouth 2 21	5 26	6 34	♋ 10	morn.	5 14
17	4	Pegaſi Mark. riſes 2 6	5 25	6 35	22	0 31	6 1
18	5	*warm and*	5 23	6 37	♌ 4	1 18	6 46
19	6	*moderate.*	5 22	6 38	16	1 58	7 35
20	7	☉ enters ♉	5 21	6 39	28	2 36	8 19
21	F	Days increaſe 4 4	5 20	6 40	♍ 10	3 10	9 2
22	2	*Flying clouds.*	5 18	6 42	22	3 41	9 44
23	3	St. George.	5 17	6 43	♎ 4	4 9	10 29
24	4	☌ ☉ ♄ oriental.	5 16	6 44	16	4 41	11 15
25	5	☌ ☉ ☿ ori. St. Mark.	5 15	6 45	29	5 30	morn.
26	6	*Expect rain*	5 14	6 46	♏ 12	riſes	0 1
27	7	*toward*	5 13	6 47	25	8 23	0 52
28	F	Bull's eye ſets 8 57	5 12	6 48	♐ 9	9 30	1 45
29	2	*the end.*	5 11	6 49	23	10 31	2 40
30	3	Pegaſi Algen. riſes 2 48	5 10	6 50	♑ 7	11 30	3 38

Information like this was given in Banneker's almanacs for every month of the year. (From the Schomburg Collection)

The letter shows that Banneker was aware of how Jefferson had changed his thinking. In the Declaration of Independence were the words "all men are created equal," but a decade later Jefferson had mentioned the inferiority of the Negro in his *Notes on Virginia* (1785).

In the letter that Banneker wrote to Jefferson, he apologized for one so humble writing to one so great, pointing out that Negroes "are looked upon with an eye of contempt; and considered rather as brutish than human, and scarcely capable of mental endowments." Even though Banneker was aware that Jefferson had expressed thoughts of that nature in his *Notes on Virginia*, Banneker said "I hope . . . that you are a man far less inflexible in sentiments of this nature, than many others . . ."

Banneker went on to affirm his own beliefs that "one universal Father hath given being to us all . . . endowed us with the same faculties . . . we are all of the same family."

With his *Almanac* as proof of what a Negro was capable of in a state of freedom, Banneker pleaded for a new attitude by Jefferson and others toward colored people:

". . . recommending to you and all others, to wean yourselves from those narrow prejudices which you have imbibed with respect to them, and as Job proposed to his friends, 'put your soul in their soul's stead'; thus shall your hearts be enlarged with kindness and benevolence towards them . . ."

Thus the brilliant Banneker protested prejudice, contrasted slavery with the demands of Americans for liberty from Britain, and pleaded for tolerance.

Jefferson's reply to Banneker was much shorter.

Philadelphia, August 30, 1791

Sir,—I thank you sincerely for your letter of the 19th instant, and for the Almanac it contained. Nobody wished more than I do to see such proofs as you exhibit, that nature has given to our black brethren, talents equal to those of the other colors of men, and that the appearance of a want of them is owing merely to the degraded condition of their existence, both in Africa and America. I can add with truth, that nobody wishes more ardently to see a good system commenced for raising the condition both of their body and mind to what it ought to be, as fast as the imbecility of their present existence, and other circumstances which cannot be neglected, will admit. I have taken the liberty of sending your Almanac to Monsieur de Condorcet, Secretary of the Academy of Sciences at Paris, and member of the Philanthropic Society, because I considered it as a document to which your color had a right for their justification against the doubts which have been entertained of them. I am, with great esteem, Sir, your most obedient humble servant.

Thos. Jefferson

That same day Jefferson wrote to the Frenchman, the Marquis de Condorcet:

I am happy to be able to inform you that we have now in the United States a Negro, the son of a black man born in Africa and of a black woman born in the United States, who is a very respectable mathematician. I procured him to be employed under one of our chief directors in the laying out of the new federal city on the Potomac, & in the interval of his leisure, while on that work, he made an Almanac for the next year, which he sent me in his own hand-writing, & which I am enclosing to you. I have seen very elegant solutions of Geometrical problems by him. Add to this that he is a worthy and respectable member of society. He is a free man. I shall be de-lighted, to see these instances of moral eminence so multiplied as to prove that the want of talents ob-served in them is merely the effect of their degraded condition, and not proceeding from any difference in the stature of the parts on which intellect depends.

Since de Condorcet and the Academy of Sciences spread his fame throughout Europe, Banneker now had world recognition as well as national. Debaters in En-gland's Parliament, men such as William Pitt, pointed to Banneker and his work as proof that the Negro was not inferior.

On Sunday, October 19, 1806, Banneker took a walk. He admired the beauty of the gold, bronze, and red leaves that covered the ground. Suddenly he collapsed. Friends carried him into the log cabin where his wooden clock still ticked rhythmically. There he died. He was almost seventy-five years old.

The newspaper, *Federal Gazette and Baltimore Daily Advertiser,* wrote:

"Mr. Banneker is a prominent instance to prove that a descendent of Africa is susceptible of as great mental improvement and deep knowledge of the mysteries of nature as that of any other nation."

So outstanding was Banneker that Marcus Conway, in an article printed during the Civil War, long after Banneker's death, wrote:

"History must record that the most original scientific mind which the South has yet produced was that of the . . . African, Benjamin Banneker."

CHAPTER 5

THE SECRET OF THE SEA
Paul Cuffe

A boy stood on a windy shore in southern Massachusetts. He was spellbound by the restless ocean.

Paul Cuffe waited impatiently for the ridge he knew would appear on the surface of the dark gray water. He was so absorbed in watching the sea that he had forgotten his sister was with him. The wave moved slowly toward the shore, towering above the boy and girl.

"It has a big white face!" Paul shouted. "It's reaching for the sky."

The giant wave crashed like thunder and the water rushed toward them.

His sister screamed. "I'm afraid!" she said, and covered her ears with thin brown hands as she ran for the nearest hill.

Paul raced after her. He saw she was trembling and reached for her hand. "Sister," he said kindly, "there is nothing to fear." His boyish voice was calm. "The ocean can't hurt you. You're not even near the water."

"I'm afraid," she repeated, her voice quivering. She held tightly to his hand. "Let's go home," she begged.

"I wish you could feel the way I do about the ocean,"

Paul Cuffe

he said. "It's wonderful. Papa and Mama bought land here because it's an island, so we have water all around us." Paul smiled at her. "We get some of our best food from the ocean, like that fish Mama baked last night."

His sister nodded.

"Someday we may even get on a big ship with white sails and go far away," Paul said, looking out at the water, now whipped by a wind from a clear sky.

"But the ocean is so big and cruel," his sister insisted. "Sometimes men are drowned."

The restless sea that made his sister afraid, seemed to give Paul strength and courage. When the waves rose high in the air with a roar, Paul was sure the ocean was trying to tell him something he should know. Other times, when the sea was as calm as glass, he looked far away to the horizon. What was beyond?

Paul continued to puzzle about the secret hidden from him hundreds of miles away on the other side of the Atlantic. He was not to understand the message of the sea until years later.

Paul Cuffe was born on a cold winter day, January 17, 1759, on Cuttyhunk Island, about seven miles from the Massachusetts coast. Discovered in 1602, Cuttyhunk is the farthest west of the Elizabeth Islands that form the southern boundary of Buzzards Bay. At the time of Paul's birth, the French and Indian War was being fought in America.

His parents were Cuffe Slocum and Ruth Moses Slocum. Paul's father was formerly the slave of Ebenezer Slocum. Then in 1742 John Slocum, a member of the family, bought him. As was customary, Cuffe took his master's name. Sometime between 1742 and

1746 Cuffe Slocum became free. By working longer hours he was able to earn his purchase price. So his descendants were free-born Negroes.

The town records of Dartmouth, Massachusetts, show that Cuffe Slocum married Ruth Moses, an Indian girl. She was probably a member of the Wampanoag, one of John Eliot's tribe of praying Indians. They both were members of the Society of Friends, better known as Quakers. They were married in their home town of Dartmouth by the Reverend Philip Taber. Later they moved to Dukes County, of which Cuttyhunk Island is a part.

Paul was the seventh child and youngest son of the ten children born to Cuffe and Ruth Slocum.

When Paul was a small boy, Cuttyhunk Island was a lonely place. There were more wild animals than people. The only house on Cuttyhunk belonged to Paul's family. Fishermen in small boats sailed along the coast.

The family had to work long hours on the farm to make a meager living. Sometimes when he had finished his chores for the day, Paul slung his fishing rod over his shoulder and headed for Buzzards Bay. The tall athletic boy was a good fisherman, so he generally returned with enough fish for supper.

Since there was no meeting house, or other church, on Cuttyhunk Island, the family had religious services on Sunday evening in the big kitchen in front of the stone fireplace.

Paul listened to his father as he sat close to the hearth, watching the logs crackle. He liked the twenty-third Psalm, the Shepherd Psalm, the family recited together:

When Paul was a small boy, Cuttyhunk Island was a lonely place.

"The Lord is my shepherd; I shall not want."

"Even though the Lord will take care of you," Paul's father warned, "you must work hard for the Lord." Then he paused, and added, "The Lord sees all of His people as His children. But many people do not see others as the Lord does." The Negro closed the Bible and studied his family. "Never forget that all your lives you will have to work harder than others to earn your living, even though you are free-born Negroes." It was not said harshly, nor was his father resentful. He was telling his sons and daughters that because they were part Indian and Negro, often they would not be accepted as equals by the white man. "Remember, my children, you are bigger than anything that can ever happen to you. But you must be strong!"

This advice was to help Paul through many trying experiences in his life.

The mother taught her children good manners, which the boy never forgot.

In 1766, when Paul was almost eight years old, his parents bought land in Dartmouth, where they had lived before they had moved to Cuttyhunk Island. This was the year of the repeal of the hated Stamp Act which had so angered the colonists in America, especially the people of Massachusetts. Since Paul's family raised most of the things they needed, they probably did not know too much about what Britain was doing to its American colonies. Also at that time Negroes in the North did not mix too easily with the white citizens in their area.

Five years later, in March 1772, when Paul was thirteen, his father died. Paul and his brother John took on much of the responsibility of the farm. By this time several of the older children had their own homes. But there was his mother to care for, as well as his three younger sisters. He later inherited the farm.

Paul had always resented the fact that his last name, Slocum, was the name of the man who had once owned his father as a slave. He persuaded his brothers and sisters to drop the name Slocum and use their father's first name, Cuffe, for their last name.

This responsibility of caring for his family and managing the farm made Paul older than his years. It also meant a great sacrifice—his dream of getting an education. At the time of his father's death, Paul had learned little more than his alphabet, but he was eager to learn more.

And more than ever he seemed determined to find out about ships. Whenever he had a free moment, he hurried to the shore to study them, their full sails filled with wind as they rode over the rough waves.

If he saw a sailor, he longed to ask him a question. Sometimes he did ask one politely. Sometimes the sailor would answer him. Other times he would hunch his shoulders and walk rudely away. When this happened, Paul sensibly realized that many sailors were from other countries and did not understand English. Often, though, he feared he was being ignored because of his dark skin.

But if a sailor took time to explain the kind of work he did on board ship, Paul was excited. The very fact that a sailor's work was risky and dangerous, especially when there were storms, made Paul more determined than ever to work on a ship.

Paul never forgot the day he had his first lesson in navigation. He had looked forward to it eagerly. At last he was going to learn about ships! He not only counted the hours, but also the minutes, he was so impatient for the lesson.

When the teacher started explaining the use of mathematics to calculate position and direction, Paul was lost. As soon as the lesson was over, Paul walked out of the room, his head down, dragging his feet, back to the farm.

His sister, Fear Phelpess, was waiting at the door.

"Paul, tell me about the lesson," she asked.

Her brother looked at her, pain written on his shiny brown face. "It was all black as midnight," he said.

Paul did not tell her that the instructor kept talking about certain principles of geometry and astronomy which he knew nothing about. He walked toward the field that needed to be plowed.

His sister caught up with him. "After a while you will understand it," she said.

"I hope so," he said, "because some day I am going to sea!"

After the second lesson, he ran all the way back to the farm in his eagerness to tell his sister about the class. "I see a little gleam of light," he said breathlessly. He studied whenever he could. After the third lesson he told his sister, "I see more light."

At the age of sixteen, part of his dream came true. This was in 1775, the first year of the American Revolution. He went as a seaman on a whaling ship bound for the Gulf of Mexico. On his second trip, he sailed to the West Indies.

On his third voyage the following year, in 1776, when he was seventeen years old, Paul was captured by the British. He was in prison in New York City for three months.

While behind bars, Paul made up his mind that, when he was released, he would study harder than ever. He was determined that some day he would own a ship. He couldn't afford to buy one, but he might build it. But if his dream was to come true, he had to know geometry.

When the British released him from prison, Paul Cuffe went to Westport, a village in Massachusetts not too many miles from his birthplace. He farmed and studied, never forgetting his dream. Whenever he sold any of his farm produce, he tried to save part of it. Slowly the leather pouch that held the coins became heavier and heavier. He hid it carefully. Sometimes he became discouraged, for he was impatient for his ship.

Three years later, in 1779, while the British and the American colonists were still at war, Paul built a boat. His brother David helped him.

Paul was certain he could make money by having his own ship. He planned to trade with the people of Connecticut who lived on the coast, some fifty miles to the southwest.

But there were many difficulties. The sea was often rough with storms, there was constant trouble with pirates. During the American Revolution, when the British and the American colonies were at war, there were no patrols protecting the coast, so pirates were able to menace all the ships on the Atlantic seaboard.

His brother David, who did not have the same in-

With the help of his brother David, Paul built his first boat.

terest and enthusiasm for the sea, told him, "It's too risky to take the ship and sail along this coast."

"Of course it's risky, but I'm willing to take a chance," Paul argued.

"It's too dangerous," David insisted. "I can't and won't risk my life on another trip."

"I can't manage the business and this ship without you," Paul said, trying to reason with his brother.

"I know that, but this is not good business," David declared. "At least I feel safe working on the farm."

So David went back to the farm.

Paul was still determined, however, to continue on the sea. He began an inspiring struggle against great odds.

If Paul had not had his dream, plus his intense love for the sea, he would not have made it. His drive kept him going, while others without a similar vision would have given up.

Paul still had the boat he and David had built together. So the following year, in 1780, he set out to sea alone. But his boat, loaded with valuable cargo, was lost in a bad storm that raged along the Connecticut coast.

Undaunted, Paul Cuffe built another boat. It was hard lonely work. At times he feared he would never finish.

The day he launched his boat, Paul's heart beat fast. He wasted no time sailing it out into the bay.

That night as his boat ran smoothly in the water, he had an uneasy feeling. Were pirates nearby? His heart sank.

In a distance a big black object was moving slowly

toward him. It could be a whale, but he feared it was a ship filled with thieves.

The brave young man prayed silently. If only there was more wind, then maybe he could get away from the pirates. That was his only chance.

Unfortunately luck was not with him on this journey. Pirates seized his boat.

There are no records telling how Paul Cuffe finally reached land. He escaped from the pirates and probably swam to shore.

When Paul finally got back to his home town, he was in despair. He certainly could not expect any sympathy from David. Perhaps it would be more sensible to give up the plan to trade along the seacoast.

Whenever he glanced at the water and the rolling waves, though, they held the same fascination for him as when he was a boy. His deep interest was still in ships.

He would take the risk for the third time.

Paul assembled the materials to build another boat. He was gratified when David offered to help him again. He also had the good fortune to borrow money to buy a cargo.

Even though the route was still dangerous, Paul dared to take the risk. He started bravely for Nantucket, some sixty miles southwest of Westport.

Pirates chased him.

In trying desperately to get away, his boat hit a rock. This time, however, the pirates did not capture him or his boat. Even though the vessel was badly damaged, he finally got back to Westport. He wasted no time, working night and day, to repair the boat.

Later he sailed to Nantucket with his cargo, but he lost money on this venture. On a second voyage to Nantucket, pirates robbed him of his cargo, beating him severely. Paul still would not give up. He set out on a third voyage to Nantucket. This time he made a profit.

When he returned, David said, "Paul, you'll be a rich man one of these days! I don't think it will be too many years, either." He looked directly at his brother. "What makes you so determined?"

"I like the sea," Paul answered. "I like to sail."

Then he turned abruptly and studied the gray turbulent water. When would he solve the mystery that the sea held?

Paul Cuffe continued to make voyages along the coast.

"If I can make some more money, I intend to buy a larger ship and hire a sailor to help me," Paul told his brother.

"You'll have them," David prophesied.

Some months later Paul purchased a ship. He also found a good seaman who was willing to be his crew. By the time the Revolutionary War ended in 1783, the hazards on the ocean were not so great. The pirates were forced to seek other waters. Paul soon started to make larger profits.

That year was important for Paul Cuffe, now twenty-four. He married Alice Pequit, an Indian girl, of the same Wampanoag tribe that his mother belonged to. The ceremony took place in Dartmouth where his parents were married.

The Cuffes had two sons, Paul Jr. and William, and six daughters. They lived in a rented house for some time, but in 1797, Paul was unusually successful. With profits from Maryland corn, he bought property. He paid $3500 for a large farm located on the west bank of the Westport River. A number of years later, he built a wharf and a storehouse. Westport was his home for the rest of his life.

In 1797, when he and his family settled in Westport, he found no schoolhouse or tutor in the neighborhood. Paul Cuffe was disturbed and troubled, for he wanted his children to have a good education. He could now afford to educate them, for he was a successful businessman.

He called a meeting of his neighbors, all white people, to help him work out a plan. Nothing was resolved at this first meeting or others that followed. Unfortunately, the people could not agree on a plan, probably because Negro and white children would be attending the same school.

At last in desperation, Cuffe built a schoolhouse on his farm with his own money. Then he offered it to the public. Cuffe also paid the teacher's salary as well as all expenses of operating the school. Negro and white students studied together.

Throughout his life, Paul Cuffe was generous with his money. He was especially interested in trying to help others get an education. He even taught navigation. Some of his apprentices were African Negroes, American Negroes, and at least one white student.

The Society of Friends was an essential part of Cuffe's life. He had been brought up in that faith, and he continued in it. In 1808, at the age of forty-nine, Paul Cuffe joined the Westport Society of Friends. He not only became a devoted worker, but occasionally spoke at Sunday services. In 1813, the Westport Friends had many more members and needed a larger building. It was an expensive project, but Paul Cuffe helped finance the new building. The meeting house cost over one thousand dollars. The records show that Paul Cuffe furnished nearly $600 worth of building materials. He probably donated most of it.

All his life, Paul Cuffe championed the rights of Negroes, working for civic privileges, denouncing slavery, and hitting at the slave trade.

Early in his career, he became involved in the struggle for Negro rights in Massachusetts. This came during the Revolutionary War, with the colonists seeking rights and liberty from Britain, but denying the same rights and liberty to Negroes living in the thirteen colonies.

In 1777 a petition was sent by Massachusetts slaves to the state legislature. It asked for a law to be passed ending slavery in the state. Since Cuffe was active in the cause of abolition, it is possible that he had something to do with this petition.

Cuffe was definitely involved in the petition of February 10, 1780, sent to the Massachusetts legislature by seven Negroes of Dartmouth, including Paul and John Cuffe. This protested taxation without representation.

Later in 1780, the Cuffe brothers petitioned the Court of General Sessions in Bristol County for relief from oppressive taxes laid on them for 1777–80, especially the last two years. They claimed to be Indians, not subject to tax. They also protested on the grounds of being Negroes who were denied representation, thus finding it hard to make a living.

The two brothers were put in jail. On June 11, 1781, John Cuffe paid 8 pounds 12 shillings to the constable. The following day, the Court of General Sessions at Taunton ordered their petition and the proceedings on it dismissed.

While their petition, resistance, and jailing did not directly bring about Negro suffrage in Massachusetts, it did aid this eighteenth-century civil rights movement. Property qualifications for voting remained until 1785. But court rulings, based on the Massachusetts Constitution of 1780, resulted in Negroes gaining civic privileges. However, no civil rights law was passed in Massachusetts as a result of their petition, as some writers have claimed.

About 1795, when Cuffe sailed to Vienna, Maryland, to load corn, the people of that town were alarmed when they saw a Negro sea captain and his crew. Some citizens were so disturbed that they organized a group to drive Paul Cuffe and his men out of town. Since Cuffe's papers were legal, this failed.

When Cuffe learned that the people of Vienna were so disturbed, he told his men:

"Maryland is a slave state, so they cannot understand that in Massachusetts Negroes are free. We must not in any way show that we are offended. Be on your best behavior. Do not insult anyone. You must be bigger than anything that can ever happen to you."

This was by far the best advice Cuffe could have given his crew. In a few days the citizens began treating Cuffe and his men with kindness and respect.

Though Cuffe had been accepted finally, he resented the fact that white captains and their crews did not have to undergo the ordeals that a crew of Negroes endured.

What could he do to make matters better for the free Negroes?

On the return trip to Massachusetts, Cuffe was irritable and cross. His men realized that an unusually serious problem was troubling him.

He spent hours gazing out at the ocean, lost in thought. Through the years, whenever he was troubled he had found peace by looking at the sea.

Powerful waves beat against the ship. All Cuffe could think of were the times he had been insulted or ignored because of his color. This hurt, because he was proud of the fact that he was a Negro.

Then Cuffe was suddenly aware that the vessel was sailing smoothly on a quiet ocean. His mind seemed clearer. He felt no resentment.

"On the other side of the Atlantic Negroes could be free," he said out loud.

Cuffe again studied the water. Then he looked toward the horizon and Africa.

Slowly the message which he had sought for years was revealed. He knew what he would do.

He would try to establish a colony for American Negroes in Africa! He would also work to help the Africans.

"My brethren, the Africans," he whispered to the ocean.

There was already a colony in Sierra Leone, West Africa. It had been started by British humanitarians, for Negroes from Canada, West Indies, and England. There were also some Negroes who had served in the British forces in the Revolution and had left with the

British armies, some going to Canada, others to England. The African Institution in London was pushing the interests of Sierra Leone, anxious for the colony to succeed, thereby discouraging the slave trade.

When Cuffe's interest in Africa became known, Americans joined the British in helping him. They saw Cuffe as a means of developing a prosperous African homeland where Negroes of America and Europe could go.

Governor Zachariah Macaulay of Sierra Leone, who was a Director of the African Institution, let Cuffe know he would be welcome.

Cuffe outlined his plans to the Westport Quakers. The Friends wrote a letter of recommendation, explaining that Cuffe's observations in Africa "would enable him to judge whether he should do right to encourage some sober families of black people in America to settle among the Africans, and if so, he intended to convey them in his own vessel."

As early as 1810, the plan had definitely matured in Cuffe's mind to aid American Negroes to settle in Africa and help the natives so they could improve their way of life.

With a crew of nine Negroes, Cuffe sailed on his brig, the *Traveller,* January 1, 1811, from Westport for Sierra Leone. When he arrived and talked to the governor, he was told that the colony had not been successful.

Then he sailed to England, where he stayed in the homes of various important people and dined with many prominent men and their families.

Paul Cuffe was tall and of a fine build. He had tact

Paul Cuffe received a warm welcome in Sierra Leone where a colony had been founded for Negroes who wanted to return to Africa.

and discretion, and he impressed the people he met in England by his dignity of manner and his piety.

Then he returned to Sierra Leone, noting possibilities for colonization and trade. He left February 1812, reaching America on April 19. The United States and England were ready to go to war. His ship was seized by a U.S. revenue cutter and condemned for bringing in a British cargo.

Cuffe traveled to Washington by coach in May 1812. He met with President James Madison. The federal authorities decided that his trip was innocent and of good intentions. His ship was returned to him and he was allowed to reclaim and sell his cargo.

Now Cuffe put more time than before in pushing his colonization plans. He formed societies of American Negroes in various cities to correspond with the Friendly Society of Sierra Leone and with the London African Institution.

Cuffe was eager to return to Sierra Leone, but the War of 1812 interfered. The United States Congress debated his petition to be allowed to carry out colonization during the War of 1812; the Senate approved but the House rejected it since he would be dealing with a colony belonging to the enemy nation, Britain. He finally sailed on the *Traveller* December 10, 1815.

On this colonization trip, the first practical demonstration of re-colonizing United States Negroes in the African homeland, he carried thirty-eight persons, eighteen adults and twenty children. The expenses of thirty of the passengers were paid by Paul Cuffe. The other eight paid for themselves. Cuffe spent over $4000 from his own savings for this trip.

The Governor and the Friendly Society in Sierra Leone treated the Americans well. The African Institution of London helped with the expenses of rations for the newcomers. Each family seems to have been given a town lot and fifty acres of land. Many of them later became leaders in the colony.

Later one of the Americans, Perry Locke, complained about being called to jury duty. Cuffe's comment was: "He complained in America because he was deprived of these privileges; and then he murmured because he was called upon." He ordered him, "Go and fill thy seat, do as well as thee can."

Cuffe, unfortunately, did not fare too well in terms of trade. The African Institution had not cleared the cargo or the extra passengers. The *Traveller* had brought tobacco, soap, flour, candles, iron for a sawmill, grindstones, nails and glass, a wagon and plow. Cuffe had realized on his previous trip how badly such items were needed. Even though the War of 1812 was over, the British government was still not permitting American ships to sail into the harbors of her colonies. This was under peace-treaty terms. For a while Cuffe feared that he would not be allowed to land his ship. But he finally got permission and paid import duties on his cargo.

Cuffe returned to the United States in May 1816, and continued to push the colonization project. The *Traveller* was kept busy freighting along the Atlantic coast and in several voyages to the West Indies. Cuffe had evidently sold the rest of his fleet, possibly to meet expenses for his African projects. Cuffe's fleet, amassed between 1793 and 1806, included: the 268-ton ship

Alpha; two brigs, the *Traveller* (109 tons) and the *Hero* (162 tons); the 69-ton *Ranger;* and the 42-ton schooner *Mary.* He owned all these vessels outright or in partnership. Despite his many philanthropies, he left a fortune of $20,000 at his death.

The following year Cuffe's health began to fail. He died at his home in Westport, September 9, 1817, during the first year of James Monroe's presidency. He was buried in the Friends' cemetery at the Old Meeting House in Westport. Almost a hundred years later, in 1913, Cuffe's great grandson, Horatio Howard, erected a five-foot granite monument in the front part of the Meeting House at Westport. Cut into the stone are the words:

In memory of Captain Cuffe, Patriot, Navigator, Educator, Philanthropist, Friend.

A fitting tribute to one of the most widely known and respected of all American Negroes.

CHAPTER 6

PIONEER TEACHER
AND PREACHER
John Chavis

A young man walked eagerly down the long corridor of Nassau Hall in Princeton, New Jersey. His bearing was erect, even noble. He had high hopes this autumn day.

John Chavis glanced at his homespun suit and straightened the coat that almost touched his knees. His strong hand tightened as he gripped the big black hat he had purchased that morning with coins saved over months.

John Chavis stood for a few minutes in front of the high oak door. He was worried about his meeting with the president of the College of New Jersey. What if Dr. John Witherspoon said no?

There was no question in John's mind what he wanted to do. He longed for able teachers to instruct him in religion and Greek and Latin. Then he would be better fitted to carry out his plan. He had heard that Dr. Witherspoon was interested in helping students of all races to get a better education.

John Chavis

The heavy-set Negro from North Carolina took a deep breath and knocked.

"Come in!" The voice was loud but not frightening.

John Chavis caught the Scottish accent. At least Dr. Witherspoon did not sound unfriendly or too formal. He turned the knob and pushed open the door.

A large man with white hair and ruddy complexion greeted him. The two talked for quite a long time, and the interview went better than John Chavis had dared to hope. He was never to forget this important day.

Dr. Witherspoon wasted no time in asking him a direct question. "Mr. Chavis, why did you come to see me?"

John Chavis did not evade the question. "Sir, I want to be a preacher and also a teacher. But I need more education." He paused a moment and his brown eyes flashed. "I want to teach boys and girls to grow up to be good citizens and Christian parents." He spoke from his heart. "Dr. Witherspoon, you are both a preacher and a teacher, and I, too, am a Presbyterian."

Dr. Witherspoon nodded. "That is a good combination," he said thoughtfully, glancing down at his clerical garb. "I always have considered myself God's minister in the sacred and civil sense."

The distinguished gentleman went on. "Then in your work you will emphasize love for one's God and loyalty to this land?"

John Chavis nodded.

"I believe that education should fit a man for public usefulness." Dr. Witherspoon spoke with determination.

John Chavis was later to learn that this man declared

that he had "become an American the moment he had landed in the thirteen colonies." Certainly there was no man more dedicated to the cause of Liberty. He had the distinction of being the only clergyman who signed the Declaration of Independence.

At one point Dr. Witherspoon commented on the excellent English Chavis used.

"I like to use the correct words when I speak," John Chavis said.

"You use American English," Dr. Witherspoon said approvingly. "This is a new country and Americans should have their own way of speaking." This was a strong belief of the reverend doctor, for he is credited with inventing the term "Americanism."

"Where do you want to preach and teach?" Dr. Witherspoon asked, as he warmed to his visitor.

"My home is in North Carolina," the heavy-set man with a life mission answered. "I was born about 1763 near Oxford in Granville County, in that state."

"Your work will not be easy," the Scotsman frankly admitted.

He did not have to tell John Chavis this, for he already realized it. Because he was a Negro, his plan would be more difficult to work out than if he had been born white. At least, he was a free-born Negro.

Dr. Witherspoon encouraged students from different backgrounds and races to study at his college; while he was president from 1768 to 1794, both Indians and Africans were students there. Undoubtedly John Chavis was one of this group. The College of New Jersey, now Princeton University, listed John Chavis as a non-grad-

"*I want to be a preacher and a teacher. I want to teach boys and girls to be good citizens. But to do this I need more education.*"

uate. Several biographers claim that he was a private student of Dr. Witherspoon's, and not enrolled in regular classes.

Records are not complete about how it happened that John Chavis came to this college in New Jersey. Some claim that Chavis was sent there to settle a bet between two southern gentlemen over whether a Negro could profit from college.

A more logical explanation is that some influential Presbyterians in North Carolina, who were impressed with Chavis' native abilities and his desire to be a minister, arranged for him to go to the Presbyterian college.

Chavis also attended Washington and Lee University, then called Liberty Hall Academy, which was in Lexington, Virginia. Chavis seldom talked about his early life, but in a letter to a good friend he once mentioned that he was a "free-born American and Revolutionary soldier." Since he was a boy in his teens when the colonists declared war against Great Britain, it is likely that he did fight in the American Revolution.

After his schooling, Chavis applied to the Presbyterian church for a license to be a minister in Lexington, Virginia.

The minutes of the Presbytery of Lexington for October 15–19, 1799, read: "John Chavis, a black man, personally known to most members of Pres. & of unquestionably good fame, and a communicant in the Presn. church, was introduced and conversed with relative to . . . his call to preach the ever lasting Gospel."

The color of his skin was not an issue. Accepting Chavis' account and feeling that "like their Heavenly

Father," the Presbytery "should be no respecter of persons," the Lexington group in its October 19 minutes "agreed, notwithstanding his colour to take him under their care for further trials in the usual form."

Almost a year later, he was assigned the subject for the sermon he was to give before the board. It was from the Acts 16:31: "Believe on the Lord Jesus Christ, and thou shalt be saved. . . ."

Chavis spent a great deal of time preparing the message for this test. He prayed for guidance. Even though those who would hear the sermon would be ministers and officials of the Presbyterian church, he was thinking of the people in the rural sections of Virginia and North Carolina to whom he would minister when he became a licensed preacher.

The slaves working hard on the plantations from dawn to sunset had little to look forward to unless they believed in the Lord and had faith. Their sad, despairing faces haunted him. Then he thought of those times when at religious gatherings they sang joyously "Praise the Lord. Hallelujah!" He would show in his sermon what Jesus Christ had suffered during His earthly ministry.

Chavis wanted this simple message of faith to show clearly in every sentence of his sermon. He would speak slowly. He would choose his words carefully, so that all would understand. He was not what is now called a "hell-fire" preacher. His message would be one of love.

Apparently his sermon was satisfactory, for on November 19, 1800, he was licensed to "preach the Gospel of Christ." The Lexington Presbytery went on record:

"hoping as he is a man of colour he may be peculiarly useful to those of his own complexion."

His greatest contribution was as a home missionary.

Actually, the Presbyterians were greatly concerned in having the gospel reach the Negroes. The minutes of September 4, 1801, of the General Assembly record a resolution appointing him: "That . . . Mr. John Chavis, a black man . . . who has been educated and licensed to preach by the Presbytery of Lexington in Virginia, be employed as a missionary among people of his own colour . . ."

A committee was set up to give him instructions and to prescribe a route. The aim in reaching the Negroes was that "the knowledge of religion among that people may be made more and more to strengthen the order of society . . ."

Chavis kept a journal, but it was lost. But the records of the General Assembly in 1802 show: "That the journal of Mr. John Chavis . . . was read in the Assembly." He appears to have executed his mission with great diligence, fidelity and prudence. He served as a missionary nine months.

Chavis was reappointed and in 1803 the General Assembly heard that the gospel was spreading rapidly "among the destitute inhabitants of our frontiers; among the blacks, and among the savage tribes." At this time the work of Chavis and other missionaries was hailed.

Although there is no record in the General Assembly records after 1807, Chavis seems to have continued as a missionary until the 1831 law forbade free Negroes preaching to slaves. Thus Chavis worked as a missionary for thirty years, from 1801 to 1831.

Chavis seems to have left Virginia to go to North Carolina about 1805. He appears to have united with the Orange Presbytery of North Carolina in 1809.

Chavis never seemed to have a regular pastorate, but he preached often in white churches.

George Wortham, an attorney, the son of Dr. James Wortham, one of Chavis' pupils, recorded impressions of Chavis' ability as a preacher. "His English was remarkably pure, contained no *negroisms; . . .* his explanations clear and concise, and his views, as I then thought and still think, entirely orthodox. He was said to have been an acceptable preacher, his sermons abounding in strong, common-sense views and happy illustrations without any effort at oratory or any sensational appeal to the passions of his hearers. He had certainly read God's Word much and meditated deeply upon it."

When its minister moved away, Chavis served for a short time as the minister at Old Providence Church, six miles from Oxford, North Carolina.

The first time he conducted the service, he had the feeling there was hostility toward him, but he prayed that through his sermons the white people would accept him. He was hurt that these people who claimed to be Christians could be so influenced by the color of the minister's skin. Apparently the barrier was too great for the church records show: "In 1824 Mr. Chavis, a colored but educated Presbyterian preacher, then living about twenty miles distant, proposed to supply for a year, but after coming a few Sundays and not receiving such familiar and hospitable entertainment as was desired and necessary, he discontinued his visits."

Even though Chavis was considered a sympathetic preacher and missionary, he won his greatest fame as an educator.

During his lifetime, Chavis was the leading influence in educating free Negroes in North Carolina. His students taught others and spread his dedication and his ideals.

At the time he taught, North Carolina like other slave states was not interested in educating the Negroes. In fact, the laws of 1831 and 1832 forbade teaching slaves. There was never a law barring the teaching of free Negroes, although public opinion frowned on it, especially from the 1830s on.

However, the Quakers, Presbyterians, Methodists, and other groups were interested in educating Negroes. The trade apprenticeship laws required an apprentice to be taught to read and write. This also aided many Negroes, for this practice became a tradition even though the law was changed in 1838.

As a leading Negro educator, there is no doubt that Chavis influenced education and literacy in North Carolina. Over 40 per cent of the free Negro adults there were literate in 1850. The largest number who could read and write were in Wake County where Chavis had taught.

But Chavis is probably even better known for teaching white students, among them the children of many prominent families. He could prepare these students for college because he knew Greek and Latin which were

John Chavis taught many white students in his school and prepared them for college. Some of them became leaders in North Carolina.

required for entrance. Some of his white pupils were to become eminent leaders of North Carolina, including congressmen, governors, physicians, lawyers, and professors.

Early in his teaching career, Chavis evidently tried to mix white and Negro pupils, but an 1808 advertisement for his school shows that he bowed to the wishes of the whites and ended this plan. Then he opened an evening school for Negroes "as he intends, for the accommodation of some of his employers, to exclude all children of color from his Day School. The evening school will commence at an hour by sun. When the white children leave the house, those of color will take their places, and continue until ten o'clock."

The ad mentioned the tuition: "The terms of teaching white children will be as usual, two and a half dollars per quarter; those of color, one dollar and three quarters. In both cases, the whole of the money is to be paid in advance to Mr. Benjamin S. King. Those who produce certificates from him of their having paid the money, will be admitted."

Chavis was concerned with character as well as letters, as is seen in the remainder of the ad: "Those who think proper to put their children under his care, may rely upon the strictest attention being paid not only to their education but to their morals which he deems an *important* part of Education."

His school was held in different places through the years, in the counties of Granville, Wake, Orange, and Chatham.

In a letter dated May 14, 1883, Professor J. H. Horner told that his father studied under Chavis, learning all he knew at the distinguished scholar's school. "Chavis was no doubt a good scholar and a good teacher, and hence was patronized by the best people in the county . . . The school was the best at that time to be found in the State."

Joseph Gales, Whig editor of *The Raleigh Register* visited Chavis' school one spring day. He apparently was quite impressed, for he printed the following account on April 19, 1830:

"On Friday last, we attended an examination of the free children of color, attached to the school of *John Chavis* . . . and we have seldom received more gratification from an exhibition of a similiar character. To witness a well regulated school, composed of this class of persons—to see them setting an example both in behavior and scholarship, which their *white* superiors might take pride in imitating, was a cheering spectacle to the philanthropist. The exercises throughout, evinced a degree of attention and assiduous care on the part of the instructor, highly creditable, and of attainment on the part of his scholars almost incredible."

All during the years that Chavis was teaching, he was also serving as a missionary in North Carolina.

Then one hot day in August, the greatest revolt in the history of American slaves occurred in the neighboring state of Virginia. It is known as the Southampton Insurrection. Nat Turner, a plowman and a fiery preacher, whose father had escaped to freedom, swore to massacre all the whites on the nearest plantations in Southampton County. Some sixty whites were killed in that county and the whole South was thrown into a panic. In retaliation, more than a hundred Negroes, innocent and guilty were killed before the rebellion was stopped.

John Chavis had never known news to travel so fast as the report of the cruel deaths of the white people by a fanatic Negro and his less than a dozen followers.

Negroes and whites talked about the tragedy. Chavis' parishioners came to him, with fear in their eyes. What would this mean? Chavis did not dare tell them that because of Nat Turner, not only slaves but free Negroes would be penalized.

It is not known whether John Chavis discussed this Negro rebellion with his white friends. But if he did, he would have told them that he was advising Negroes to continue to serve their masters. He never encouraged them to revolt. In fact, he opposed abolitionists and emancipation.

In a letter Chavis wrote in April 1836, he said:

"That Slavery is a national evil no one doubts, but what is to be done? It exists and what can be done with it? All that can be done, is to make the best of a bad bargain. For I am clearly of the opinion that immediate emancipation would be to entail the greatest earthly curse upon my brethren . . . I suppose if they knew I said this they would be ready to take my life, but as I wish them well, I feel no disposition to see them any more miserable than they are."

North Carolina did not need to fear or to bar his preaching. But he and other fine Negro preachers were inevitably penalized. The uprising led to more stringent slave laws in the South and to the end of societies that had been working to free the slaves. But for Chavis, it meant that this 1831 law forbade him and other free

Negroes to preach to slaves. It also meant that he could not teach slaves. The punishment was thirty-nine lashes for each offense. This law seems to have ended Chavis' career as a minister and missionary.

The law worked a great hardship on this kindly, dedicated scholar and minister. He was then close to seventy years of age. He had been dependent on the income from his preaching to supplement the small amount he received from his schools.

Chavis had a great deal of pride, but he was desperate. He also had a wife to support.

The following spring, in April 1832, Chavis wrote to the Orange Presbytery. In his letter he stated his difficulties and embarrassments as a consequence of the act that had been passed "forbidding the free people of color to preach."

The Presbytery resolution recommended Chavis' "acquiesence in the decision of the Legislature . . . until God . . . shall open to him the path of duty, in regard to the exercise of his ministry."

From 1832 until his death in 1838, the Orange Presbytery helped support Chavis.

The semiannual assessments were made on each church in the Presbytery ranging from seventy-five cents for the New Hope church to two dollars for the Hillsborough church. The Presbytery urged churches to pay promptly sums pledged "for the support of this aged laborer in the Lord's vineyard."

At the time Chavis was a minister and teacher, free slaves in the South were almost outcasts and most white people deliberately tried to ignore them, for they felt that the presence of free Negroes made the slaves

discontented. Most of the time free Negroes were iso-
lated both from the slaves as well as from the white
people. Dr. John Hope Franklin, a present-day Negro
historian, has noted the "unwritten agreements among
the white citizens that their open contact with free Negroes should be as little as possible."

Chavis, however, was an outstanding exception to
this rule in the South. His pupils, such as Horner,
boarded with him. He visited his students and also
boarded them.

Stephen B. Weeks, who married the granddaughter
of State Senator Willie P. Mangum, one of those students, wrote that when Chavis visited Mangum's home,
he "was treated with all deference and courtesy, so
much so that it caused astonishment and questioning
on the part of the younger children, which was met in
turn by 'Hush, child, he is your father's friend.'"

Paul C. Cameron, one of the wealthiest men in North
Carolina in the 1880s, wrote in a letter, April 24, 1883,
that when Chavis visited the home of his father, Judge
Cameron, "he was received by my father and treated
with kindness and consideration, and respected as a
man of education, good sense, and most estimable character. He seemed familiar with the proprieties of social
life."

Most important, Chavis showed throughout his life
that an educated Negro can compete on equal terms
with white people. Chavis did not move solely in a
Negro world. Instead, he successfully vied with, and
walked as an equal among the white leaders of his day.
As Stephen Weeks remarked, when a man like Chavis
born among an aristocratic, slaveholding society "de-

velops such intellectual power and force of character as to command, despite race and social position, not a grudging but a cheerful recognition from the exclusive aristocracy among whom he lives, he can well be pointed to as a source of inspiration and help to all future generations of his people . . ."

Hence, Chavis was highly important in the early nineteenth century, for he showed that the path for the Negro lay not in emigrating back to Africa, but in developing intellectually so as to win respect.

One historian has written: "His contemporaries . . . revered him for his fervent piety as a Christian, and respected him for his eminent ability as a teacher and preacher."

Today Chavis' accomplishments are memorialized in Raleigh, North Carolina, by a large recreational park and a federal housing project which bear his name.

INDEX

Index